ON THE ROAD WITH

The

COOKING LADIES

Let's Get Grilling

ON THE ROAD WITH

The

COOKING LADIES

Let's Get Grilling

PHYLLIS HINZ & LAMONT MACKAY

whitecap

Whitecap Books is known for its expertise in the cookbook
market, and has produced some of the most innovative and
familiar titles found in kitchens across North America. Visit
our website at www.whitecap.ca.

EDITORS: Jordie Yow and Jackie Wong
DESIGN: Andrew Bagatella
FOOD PHOTOGRAPHY: Jonathan Bielaski, Phyllis Hinz,
and Lamont Mackay
TRAVEL PHOTOGRAPHY: Phyllis Hinz and Lamont Mackay
FOOD STYLING: Tara Ballantyne, Phyllis Hinz,
and Lamont Mackay
PROOFREADER: Patrick Geraghty

Printed in Canada

Library and Archives Canada Cataloguing in Publication

Hinz, Phyllis, 1946-, author
  On the road with the cooking ladies : let's get grilling /
Phyllis Hinz and Lamont Mackay.

ISBN 978-1-77050-297-0 (paperback)

1. Barbecuing. 2. Cookbooks. 3. Hinz, Phyllis,
1946---Travel--Anecdotes. 4. Mackay, Lamont,
1945- --Travel--Anecdotes. I. Mackay, Lamont,
1945-, author II. Title.

TX840.B3H55 2017   641.7'6
C2016-900625-5

We acknowledge the financial support of the Government of
Canada through the Canada Book Fund (CBF) for our publish-
ing activities and the Province of British Columbia through the
Book Publishing Tax Credit.

Nous reconnaissons l'appui financier du gouvernement du
Canada et la province de la Colombie-Britannique par le Book
Publishing Tax Credit.

17 18 19 20 21 22   6 5 4 3 2 1

Lives touch by chance, by birth, by circumstance.
This book is dedicated to all of you who are on this journey with us.

TABLE OF CONTENTS

TRAVEL STORIES & RECIPES

INTRODUCTION

HOW DO TWO university friends with no experience in the food business become successful restaurant owners, culinary travel writers, and cookbook authors?

We quit our teaching and banking careers to travel the world, but ran out of money before ever leaving North America. We landed jobs operating a country-hotel kitchen and saved just enough for a nine-month, 25,000-kilometer European adventure in a Volkswagen van. By the time we returned to Canada, we knew we were natural nomads hooked on food, travel, and writing about our adventures. However, our travel wings were clipped because we were broke again.

We bought a restaurant as a means of income to finance future travels. One restaurant lead to another, and another, and a catering company. We were having so much fun working seven days a week in the food business that we put travel on hold for the next 20 years.

Tragedy struck with the sudden, unexpected death of Susan Emmott, our young business partner and friend. We were devastated. We sold our businesses, our houses, and all our stuff, and bought a motor home to begin an amazing nine-year, full-time, RV odyssey on the highways and backroads of North America, just to see where life would take us.

We've stood at the Arctic Circle with snowflakes falling on our faces, walked ghost towns in New Mexico, watched wild horses run among the dunes in the Carolinas, chilled our drinks with 10,000-year-old iceberg bits in Newfoundland and Labrador, walked on lava beds to the sea in Hawaii, straddled an earthquake fault line in California, and eaten our way around the Gulf of Mexico.

Our adventures on the road led to spin-off careers as food columnists, cookbook authors, travel writers, event speakers, and restaurant consultants. They also brought forward a new persona for us: The Cooking Ladies.

On the lonely road between Ludlow and Needles, California, we drove across the Mojave Desert and a trucker spoke to us on our CB radio. "What do you Cooking Ladies cook?" he asked after reading our website address (www.thecookingladies .com) on the back of our motorhome.

We told him we were writing a cookbook. Doing research. He told us he learned to cook from his grandmother. He shared his grandmother's advice with us: "If you put things you like together, it comes out good and the dish always leaves the table empty." We couldn't have said it better.

These days, when we are not on the road we are in our test kitchen, adding a pinch of this and a dash of that to cook up culinary travelogues like the ones you will find in this book. *On the Road with The Cooking Ladies: Let's Get Grilling* is a selection of our North American road trip stories paired with our grilling and smoking recipe creations. We're happy to have you join us on our culinary journey.

Our appetite for adventure continues. Interesting people, fascinating towns, and new recipes are always just a bend in the road away.

HOT TIPS FROM THE COOKING LADIES

KEEP IT CLEAN!

The easiest way to clean a gas grill is to turn the temperature to high, close the lid, and let it heat for 10–15 minutes. This will char food remnants, making them easier to scrape off with a wire brush.

KEEP IT OILED!

Oiling the grill grate before each use helps to prevent food from sticking. This also helps to clean the grate by removing dark residue, black specks, and pieces of metal that could be left behind by a wire brush. We preheat the grill first and then oil it. With a pair of long-handled tongs, we rub oiled paper towel over the entire grate. We use canola oil but any oil that will tolerate high heat will work.

KEEP IT HOT!

High heat sterilizes the grates. When grilling meat, a clean, hot grill seals in the juices, creates nice grill marks, and makes the meat less likely to stick. Start with a hot grill and set the temperature to the recipe specifications. Unless the recipe states otherwise, cooking with the lid closed helps to regulate the grill temperature and creates a smokier flavor. The food will also cook faster and use less fuel.

HOW TO CREATE DIAMOND GRID MARKS ON A STEAK

To put those diamond grid marks on a steak or a chop, make sure the grate is hot and well-oiled so the meat doesn't stick. Place the meat on the hot, oiled grate at a 45-degree angle. Sear, then rotate the meat to a 45-degree angle the opposite way without turning the steak over. When the meat has diamond grid marks on the first side, turn it over and repeat the angle trick. Cook to desired doneness.

GETTING ORGANIZED

For efficiency, we gather any necessary supplies together before we begin to grill: tongs, lifters, basting sauce, basting brush, oven mitts, thermometer, wet soapy cloth, oil, paper towels, timer, clean plate for cooked meat, cold drinks, and sunscreen for the cook.

PREPARING WOODEN SKEWERS FOR THE GRILL

When we grill kabobs we like metal skewers, but wooden skewers work just as well if they are soaked in water for at least 30 minutes prior to using them. This delays any burning.

PREVENTING FLARE-UPS

Flare-ups—unexpected and unwanted flames— are often caused by the fat content in meat, grease build-up, or high heat. Trimming excess fat from meat helps to prevent flare-ups. When a flare-up occurs, turn heat down or temporarily move food to a cooler side of the grate. Instead of using water to control flames, sprinkle on a small amount of baking soda.

COOKING OVER INDIRECT HEAT

We set the grill on indirect heat to cook dishes we would normally bake in the oven in the test kitchen. The indirect cooking method is good for large cuts of meat that require long cooking times at lower temperatures. First we preheat the grill with all burners, then we turn one side off and place the food on the grate over the unlit burner. When using the indirect cooking method, the grill lid must remain closed as much as possible to create an oven effect. Every time the lid is opened, heat will be lost and cooking time will be extended. For indirect cooking, we prefer a digital temperature probe to monitor the cooking process; however, an ovenproof meat thermometer can be used. The thermometer goes into the meat at the beginning of the cooking time and can stay there during the entire cooking process. The advantage of the digital thermometer probe is that it allows you to read the internal temperature of the meat from outside the grill without lifting the lid.

GRILLING ACCESSORIES

A multi-purpose grill topper is ideal for cooking delicate meats, vegetables, and seafood, and for preventing smaller food items from falling through the grate.

A cast iron griddle is used for frying food like bacon and fish. It's also useful for cooking foods that spread, such as pancakes and eggs.

A porcelain wok, either solid or with holes, is used for stir-frying or cooking small pieces of food that would normally fall through the grate.

SAFE FOOD HANDLING TIPS

- Never leave food sitting out of the refrigerator for more than two hours or, in hot weather, less than an hour.
- Wash hands with soap before handling any food and especially after handling raw meat.
- Disinfect cutting boards and counters that have come in contact with raw meat.
- Do not put raw meat and cooked meat on the same plate or in contact with each other.
- Never allow uncooked meat to come in contact with food that will be eaten raw, such as a salad.
- Discard marinades after use. Any meat marinade that is not discarded needs to be boiled for 10 minutes before using in order to destroy any bacteria.
- Thaw frozen meat in the refrigerator, never at room temperature.
- Always cook ground meat all the way through to the center to kill any harmful bacteria.

GRILL START-UP AND SHUT-OFF TIPS

Always open the lid before lighting a gas grill. If you smell gas, shut it off and check for leaks. Don't forget to turn off both the gas and the grill knobs when the grill is not in use.

INTERNAL TEMPERATURE GUIDE

THE INTERNAL TEMPERATURE, rather than the cooking time, is the best method to determine when meat is cooked. Cooking time increases in cold and windy weather. The number of times and duration that the lid is opened also impact the performance of the grill.

An instant-read thermometer registers the internal temperature instantly and is designed to be used toward the end of the cooking time and not to be left in the meat. The thermometer is to be inserted into the thickest part of the meat, not touching fat or bone.

Another handy gadget is a digital probe meat thermometer that can be read from outside the grill. We like this for larger cuts of meat because we don't have to open the lid.

BEEF AND LAMB
- 125–130°F (52–54°C) for rare
- 135–140°F (57–60°C) for medium rare
- 145–150°F (63–66°C) for medium
- 155–160°F (68–71°C) for medium well
- 160–165°F (71–74°C) for well done

THE STEAK FINGER-POKE TEST
A rare steak will feel soft to the touch. A medium steak will yield slightly to the touch. A well-done steak will feel firm.

PORK
- 160°F (71°C) for pork roasts and chops
- 200°F (95°C) for pulled pork

POULTRY
- 165°F (74°C) in the breast
- 175°F (80°C) in the thigh

GROUND BEEF, GROUND LAMB, OR GROUND PORK
- 160°F (71°C)

GROUND CHICKEN OR GROUND TURKEY
- 165°F (74°C)

HOW TO TURN A GAS GRILL INTO A SMOKER

Grills and smokers come in every imaginable size, shape, style, and price range. The ideal is to have both a grill and a smoker. For convenience, because it's what we like and know best, we have used either a gas grill or a pellet smoker to create our recipes in this book.

A gas grill can be turned into a smoker using the following method:

1. Soak wood chips for at least 30 minutes.
2. Place the wet wood chips in a smoker box or a heavy-duty foil packet with holes poked in the top. Place this underneath one side of the cooking grate.
3. With the lid closed, preheat both sides of the grill on high for about 10 minutes or until the wood chips begin to smoke.
4. Using a pair of long-handled tongs, oil the grate by wiping it with a piece of folded paper towel dipped lightly in canola oil.
5. Reduce the heat to medium on the side with the wood chips. Turn the heat off on the side without the wood chips.
6. Place the meat on the unlit side.
7. Set the heat to the desired temperature of the recipe.

Keep the lid closed except to add extra wet wood chips and to check the meat.

SNACKS & STARTERS

Fisheries Museum of the Atlantic

ANYONE WHO HAS visited the waterfront of Lunenburg, Nova Scotia, will recognize the brilliant red buildings of the Fisheries Museum of the Atlantic. Two historic ships and five buildings make up the complex that commemorates the fishing heritage of Atlantic Canada.

The Cape Sable is a steel-hulled trawler. We were impressed with the raised railings on the galley table and cook's stove, put in place to keep the dishes and the pots and pans from flying around in rough seas. The *Theresa E. Connor,* a fishing schooner, was tied up next door. She was the last dory schooner to fish from the area. Her job was to transport fishermen out to deeper fishing waters. Once there, the men launched smaller dories on rough seas to bait their hooks and set their lines.

Inside the museum we viewed both fresh and saltwater aquariums, and we learned about whales, lobster traps, shipbuilding, and rumrunning, as well as how to tie knots and mend nets. We wandered the extensive collection of fishing artifacts and gained an appreciation for life in a fishing community.

Naturally, we gravitated to the Old Fish Factory restaurant. Looking out over the wharf, we ordered a seafood starter of mackerel, salmon, and herring—the fruits of the sea.

The cubes of salmon had a rich maple flavor, and we enjoyed them so much that we created our own version to be served as a snack or starter (see next page).

MAPLE SALMON CUBES

¾ lb (375 g) salmon fillets

½ cup (125 mL) maple syrup

2 Tbsp (30 mL) dark rum

REMOVE ANY SKIN from the salmon fillets. Trim away any dark spots. Cut the salmon into 1-inch (2.5 cm) cubes.

In a bowl, combine the maple syrup and dark rum. Stir well.

Marinate the salmon cubes in the maple syrup mixture for 1–2 hours in the refrigerator.

Place a griddle on the grill grate. Preheat the grill on medium-high (450–550°F/230–290°C) for 10 minutes with the lid closed.

Pour and spread approximately 2 Tbsp (30 mL) canola oil on the griddle. Turn the heat to medium-low.

Place the salmon cubes side by side on the griddle. Keeping the grill lid open, spoon or brush some of the marinade over the cubes. Don't let the griddle dry around the salmon. Continue to spoon the marinade over the cubes as they cook.

After about 5 minutes turn the salmon cubes over. Spoon more marinade on the griddle to keep the salmon moist. Turn and baste the salmon for another 5 minutes or until both sides are golden brown and the marinade is caramelizing around the salmon cubes. Remove the salmon before the marinade becomes dark and bitter. Serve with toothpicks.

Peace Among the Grapes

AS OUR GROUP of travel writers waited to meet the owner of Jules J. Berta Winery, a biker drove into the parking lot. He wore faded blue jeans, sunglasses, and a sleeveless vest over a tee that did nothing to hide his tanned, muscled arms.

"I'm Jules Berta. Welcome to our winery," he said.

Jules Berta Sr., his father, emigrated from Hungary and settled in Albertville, Alabama, growing grapes on the side. After serving in the US military, Jules Jr. returned to the small southern town to grow grapes with his father.

"You are going to make your own happiness. It doesn't matter what you do. If you have a passion the world will come to you," his father told him.

After the death of his father, Jules found that passion in making wine from 5 acres (2 hectares) of grapes on a 22-acre (9 hectares) farm, a property he owns with his wife, Becky. Together they control the entire process from vine to bottle. Jules tends his vines daily. He grafts new varieties and utilizes severe pruning to control inevitable diseases.

Because Jules wants to "pay for the farm and keep the lights on," he produces several sweet fruit wines for novice drinkers: Southern Thang, Born Dixie, Sassy Frass, and I Love Bubba. He knows his customers will gradually develop a palate and progress toward chardonnays and merlots and perhaps even his Green Hungarian, a white wine that affirms the Berta family history.

"You know what, my father was right. I wish he were here. I have found peace and serenity among the plants. We all need a little of that in our lives," Jules said.

The Jules J. Berta Green Hungarian white wine would pair perfectly with our Three-Pepper Antipasto recipe (see next page).

THREE-PEPPER ANTIPASTO

1 large green bell pepper

2 large red bell peppers

1 large yellow bell pepper

Extra-virgin olive oil
(for brushing)

1 cup (250 mL) sun-dried tomatoes
in oil, drained

½ tsp (2 mL) dried basil leaves

¼ cup (60 mL) extra-virgin olive oil

¼ cup (60 mL) balsamic vinegar

¼ tsp (1 mL) salt

½ tsp (2 mL) pepper

1 cup (250 mL) fresh or canned sweet
cherries

Crackers (for serving)

CUT THE PEPPERS in half lengthwise and remove the seeds. Brush the skin lightly with olive oil.

Preheat the grill on high (550–600°F/290–315°C) for 10 minutes with the lid closed.

Arrange the peppers on the grate, cavity side up. Grill the peppers with the lid closed until the skins are blistered and blackened.

Remove peppers from the grate and set aside to cool.

Finely chop the sun-dried tomatoes. Set aside.

In a large bowl, combine the basil, oil, vinegar, salt, and pepper.

Cut the cherries into quarters, removing any pits.

Add the sun-dried tomatoes and cherries to the balsamic vinegar mixture.

When the peppers are cool enough to touch, remove and discard the charred skins. Cut peppers into small cubes. Mix pepper cubes into the tomato-cherry mixture.

Transfer the antipasto to a sealed container and refrigerate overnight to blend the flavors.

Serve with crackers.

Rumrunners and Prohibition in the Windsor–Detroit Funnel

THE RUM RUNNERS Tour in Windsor, Ontario, is a travelling play depicting real people who walked the streets and worked the whiskey during the wild, crazy time of Prohibition in the 1920s and early 1930s.

Alcohol was illegal in the United States but in Ontario, Canada, it could be consumed, stashed away for medicinal purposes, or enjoyed on a whisky break at work. Exporting alcohol to America was profitable—if a person could get it there. To escape the wrath of the local police and customs officials, bootleggers and rumrunners had to be creative. Bottles were strapped to bodies, large overcoats were lined with bottle-sized pockets, and hot water bottles were filled with something other than water. Women creatively hid bottles of booze in baby buggies and stuffed them into their stockings.

In the summertime, rum-running ferries and speedboats transporting liquor to the United States were faster and better than government boats. In the winter, traffic on the frozen Detroit River was congested with skaters, sleds, and overloaded automobiles. The distance isn't far. It is said that a good center-fielder could throw a baseball across the river from Windsor to Detroit.

The Women's Temperance Movement worked to rid society of "drunken men spewing foul language" and "rouge-faced tarts" often declaring that "Lips that touch whiskey won't touch ours."

Rum was the original commodity during American Prohibition, but because it was so cheap, and generated only small profits, rumrunners turned to the more lucrative Canadian whiskey market.

Our Sherry-Marinated Shrimp recipe (see next page) would be a clever way to smuggle sherry across the border.

SHERRY-MARINATED SHRIMP

12–16 large raw shrimp, peeled and deveined

3 Tbsp (45 mL) peanut oil, divided

¾ tsp (4 mL) prepared mustard

2 Tbsp (30 mL) sherry

1 Tbsp (15 mL) red wine vinegar

Pinch of salt

Pinch of white pepper

PLACE THE SHRIMP in a bowl and toss with 1 Tbsp (15 mL) peanut oil.

Preheat the grill on high (550–600°F/290–315°C) for 10 minutes with the lid closed. Place a grill topper on the grate. Reduce heat to medium-high (450–550°F/230–290°C). Oil the grill topper by wiping it with a piece of folded paper towel dipped in peanut oil.

Cook the shrimp on the grill topper, with the lid open, for about 1–2 minutes on each side or until they turn pink. Do not overcook.

In a bowl, combine the mustard, sherry, vinegar, 2 Tbsp (30 mL) peanut oil, salt, and white pepper. Mix well.

Add the cooked shrimp to the mustard-sherry marinade. Stir, cover, and refrigerate for 1–2 hours before serving.

Remove the shrimp from the marinade and place on a serving dish.

The Promise of Colossal Shrimp

PUERTO PEÑASCO, MEXICO, otherwise known as Rocky Point, is a fishing village of 60,000 people on the Sea of Cortez. Fellow travelers whetted our appetites with tales of the gargantuan, fresh shrimp that make Rocky Point a destination. To demonstrate the size of the shrimp, they held up a hand and stretched their thumbs and forefingers as wide as possible.

We booked an overnight bus trip from Arizona to Puerto Peñasco. We took a cooler along to purchase shrimp to take home.

In the center of town, along the seawall, there was a statue of a fisherman riding a colossal shrimp, like a rodeo cowboy.

At Maria Bonita's restaurant we settled at a small table overlooking the sea and ordered Rocky Point Shrimp Cocktails. Oversized goblets arrived with the largest shrimp we had ever seen in a gazpacho-type soup made with a tomato-based broth, finely diced vegetables, and diced jalapeno for a bit of heat. A wedge of lime rested on the rims of the glasses, ready to squeeze.

The next day, a fisherman arrived in the hotel parking lot with his morning's catch in the back of a pickup truck. Plastic pails of different colors held different sized shrimp. We filled our cooler with several sizes, including Big Blues that weighed in at 14 to the pound.

We could not wait to create our own version of the Rocky Point Shrimp Cocktail (see next page).

ROCKY POINT SHRIMP COCKTAIL

12 jumbo raw shrimp, peeled and deveined

Olive oil (for tossing)

½ cup (125 mL) peeled and finely diced cucumber

½ cup (125 mL) finely diced celery

½ cup (125 mL) finely diced sweet onion

1 small jalapeno pepper, seeds and membrane removed, finely diced

½ cup (125 mL) finely diced red bell pepper

½ cup (125 mL) finely diced green bell pepper

½ cup (125 mL) finely diced avocado

1 tsp (5 mL) hot sauce

¼ cup (60 mL) fresh lime juice

2 cups (500 mL) Clamato juice (clam-tomato juice)

4–6 lime wedges

Soda crackers (for serving)

PLACE THE SHRIMP in a bowl. Toss the shrimp with olive oil.

Place a grill topper on the grill grate. Preheat the grill on medium-high (450–550°F/230–290°C) for 10 minutes with the lid closed. Oil the grill topper.

Place the shrimp on the grill topper and cook, with the lid open, about 2–3 minutes per side or until the shrimp become firm and pink. Do not overcook. Refrigerate to cool.

In a large bowl, combine the cucumber, celery, onion, peppers, avocado, hot sauce, lime juice, and Clamato juice.

Ladle the mixture into 4–6 cocktail glasses.

Add 2–3 shrimp to each glass. Use a spoon to push the shrimp down into the liquid.

Refrigerate the shrimp cocktails until ready to serve.

Serve with a lime wedge and soda crackers.

MEDITERRANEAN FUSION APPETIZER

2 large red bell peppers

6 Tbsp (90 mL) feta cheese, crumbled

½ cup (125 mL) pitted kalamata olives, cut in half

2 Tbsp (30 mL) small capers, drained

1 Tbsp (15 mL) extra-virgin olive oil + extra (for brushing)

Crackers (for serving)

PREHEAT THE GRILL on high (550–600°F/290–315°C) for 10 minutes with the lid closed.

Cut peppers in half lengthwise and remove the seeds. Lightly brush the outside skin of the peppers with olive oil.

Arrange the peppers on the grate, cavity side up. Grill the peppers until the skins are blistered and blackened, approximately 10–15 minutes with the lid closed.

Remove the peppers from the grate and set them aside to cool. When the peppers are cool, peel and discard the blackened skin. Dice the peppers.

Combine the peppers, cheese, olives, and capers in a bowl. Mix well. Add the oil and mix again.

Serve with crackers.

HOT & SWEET WINGS

16 whole chicken wings

¾ cup (185 mL) hot sauce, divided

5 tsp (25 mL) garlic powder

¼ tsp (1 mL) pepper

2 tsp (10 mL) dried oregano leaves

1 tsp (5 mL) paprika

1 tsp (5 mL) chili powder

½ tsp (2 mL) cayenne pepper

2 tsp (10 mL) dried rosemary leaves, crumbled

2 cups (500 mL) brown sugar

½ cup (125 mL) white vinegar

RINSE THE CHICKEN wings and pat them dry with paper towels. Remove and discard the wing tips.

Place the wings in a large bowl. Brush the wings with ½ cup (125 mL) of the hot sauce.

In a bowl, combine the garlic powder, pepper, oregano, paprika, chili powder, cayenne, and rosemary. Place the dry mixture in a large resealable plastic bag.

Add the coated wings to the dry mixture in the bag. Shake and toss the wings to coat them with the dry mixture. Place the bag in the refrigerator for 1–2 hours.

In a bowl, combine the brown sugar, vinegar, and remaining ¼ cup (60 mL) hot sauce. Stir until the sugar is dissolved. Set aside.

Prepare the grill for indirect cooking. Preheat only one side of the grill on high (550–600°F/290–315°C) for 10 minutes with the lid closed. Using a pair of long-handled tongs, oil the grate on the unlit side by wiping it with a piece of folded paper towel dipped in canola oil.

Place the wings on the unlit side of the grate. Reduce the heat to low (250–300°F/120–150°C).

Cook the wings for about 1½ hours with the lid closed. Rotate and baste the wings every 15 minutes with the brown sugar mixture.

Springtime at the Sugar Shack

THE PROVINCES OF Ontario and Quebec and the state of Vermont are the largest producers of maple syrup. Sugar maples are unique to the southeastern part of Canada and the northeastern area of the United States. The sap begins to flow through the trunks of sugar maple trees in the early spring, when cool nights turn into warm sunny days with temperatures above freezing.

It is believed that the First Nations people taught early North American settlers how to harvest the sap. For generations, families collected it by drilling holes into the trunks of trees and inserting small spouts. Sap buckets were hung over the spouts for collection. Some people still use buckets. Others utilize gravity and plastic tubing to take the sap from the trees directly to a storage tank.

Smoke drifting up through the fresh, cold air makes it easy to spot a sugar shack in the bush. Inside, the sap is boiled in an evaporator to eliminate water content. The resulting hot, silky, maple syrup is filtered and bottled. If left to boil down further, the syrup turns into the denser textures of maple sugar, maple butter, and maple taffy.

Maple syrup is expensive because it can take 40 gallons of sap to make a single gallon of syrup. The maple syrup season is short, lasting three to six weeks. Once the buds hit the trees, sugaring is over.

MAPLE BACON ONION RINGS

2–3 medium-sized mild onions

6 thinly sliced bacon strips

2 Tbsp (30 mL) maple syrup

1 tsp (5 mL) fresh lemon juice

1 tsp (5 mL) Dijon mustard

PEEL AND SLICE the onions into thick (½ inch/1 cm) slices widthwise.

Push out the center 2–3 rings of each onion slice. Keep the remaining outer rings together. Set the inner rings aside for another recipe.

Wind and stretch a bacon strip around each set of outer onion rings, covering the surface of the onion with the bacon. Secure the bacon ends with a toothpick.

Place the bacon-wrapped onion rings side by side in a flat baking dish.

In a bowl, combine the maple syrup, lemon juice, and mustard.

Brush the maple syrup mixture over the bacon onion rings. Cover and refrigerate for 1 hour.

Preheat the grill on medium-high (450–550°F/230–290°C) for 10 minutes with the lid closed. Using a pair of long-handled tongs, oil the grate by wiping it with a piece of folded paper towel dipped lightly in canola oil.

Place the bacon onion rings on the grate. Cook over medium-high heat with the lid closed, turning every 3–4 minutes until the bacon is cooked and the onion is tender-crisp.

Remove the toothpicks before serving.

The Colony of Avalon

THE COLONY OF Avalon is located in Ferryland, a one-hour drive south from St. John's along the east coast of Newfoundland and Labrador. The ongoing archaeological dig at the Colony is proving that the permanent European settlement in the area dates back to the early 1600s.

Standing on the shoreline of the Colony, it was easy for us to see why the Europeans settled there. The wide harbor and surrounding hill offered an ideal location for defense. The cobblestones on the beach were, and still are, naturally perfect for drying fish and building streets.

Over a million artifacts have been found at an average rate of 3,000 per week. Excavations at the Colony of Avalon take place for 20 weeks each summer. Grape seeds, gold rings, pottery, cannon balls, and other treasures are on display in the Interpretation Center. In earlier times both adults and children smoked because smoking was thought to not only keep a person warm but expand the lungs. Tobacco pipes were such a popular item that they help to date an archeological site. The older the pipe, the smaller the pipe bowl.

In the Colony's 17th century kitchen, we caught a glimpse of home life. There were no forks for eating. Forks were for feeding hay to the animals. Most meals were stews. The staples were bread, cheese, and ale. Cold water was believed to be unhealthy. Gardens were cultivated for herbs and medicines.

Our garlic bread recipe (see next page), with herbs and cheese, would fit right in with the Colony's basic diet.

CHEESY GARLIC BREAD

1 French baguette

6 Tbsp (90 mL) butter

¾ tsp (4 mL) garlic powder

1 Tbsp (15 mL) finely chopped fresh parsley

½ cup (125 mL) shredded cheddar cheese

¼ cup (60 mL) grated Parmesan cheese

CUT THE BAGUETTE into ½–¾ inch (1–2 cm) wide slices, on an angle, but not all the way through. Leave the bottom crust intact so that each slice can be easily broken away when served.

Place the butter in a bowl and soften to a spreadable stage. Mix in the garlic powder and parsley.

Place a large piece of heavy aluminum foil on the counter. Lightly brush the foil with canola oil. Transfer the loaf of bread to the center of the foil by holding the slices together while lifting.

Spread the garlic butter onto both sides of each slice of bread and on the entire top crust.

Sprinkle the cheddar cheese between each slice. Sprinkle the Parmesan cheese along the buttered top of the baguette. Tightly wrap the foil around the baguette.

Preheat the grill on medium (350–450°F/175–230°C) for 10 minutes with the lid closed. Place the garlic bread package on the grate for about 12 minutes, lid closed. Turn the package at 4-minute intervals.

Remove from heat and serve.

Promenade Through History in Quebec

WE STEPPED ONTO the cobblestone streets of Place-Royale in Old Quebec City, the only fortified city in North America and the site where Champlain began the French colonization of North America in 1608. Tourists from around the world were wandering the winding, narrow alleyways, flowing in and out of the low, antique doorways of the myriads of small shops. Just as in Europe, waiters delivered trays of cheese, fresh bread, and wine to patrons lounging at shaded tables of outdoor cafés. Photogenic flowerpots and shop signs provided color to the surrounding thick, stone walls of the city.

We rode a glass elevator up the 328-foot (100 meter) high bluff to the Upper Town where we dodged tour buses, skirted horse-drawn carriages, and strolled around Chateau Frontenac along the Dufferin Terrace, an immense boardwalk overlooking the old town. The St. Lawrence River, below, was the same waterway that provided a path for explorers hundreds of years ago. Another boardwalk, the Governor's Promenade, follows the clifftop to the National Battlefields Park outside the city walls. The park encompasses the Plains of Abraham where the British and French armies of General James Wolfe and Louis-Joseph de Montcalm-Gozon, the Marquis de Montcalm, fought in 1759.

The British won the battle but Quebec continues to maintain its French heritage. The history, architecture, and cuisine of Old Quebec City entice us back, again and again.

HOT PEPPER JELLY BRIE

1 Tbsp (15 mL) extra-virgin olive oil

1 tsp (5 mL) dried oregano leaves

12 oz (340 g) Brie wheel

1 Tbsp (15 mL) hot pepper jelly

1 Tbsp (15 mL) crushed, blanched almond slices (optional)

Crackers (for serving)

IN A SMALL bowl, combine the olive oil and oregano.

Cut the top skin off the Brie wheel. Pre-cut the Brie wheel into 16 wedges, keeping the original shape of the wheel. Cut 2 large squares of heavy-duty aluminum foil and place one square on top of the other. Make sure that the foil square is larger than the Brie wheel. Place the Brie wheel in the center of the foil.

Brush the top and sides of the brie wheel with the olive oil mixture.

Spread the hot pepper jelly on top of the brie. Sprinkle the crushed almonds over the jelly.

Preheat the grill on high (550–600°F/290–315°C) for 10 minutes with the lid closed.

Turn the heat off on one side of the grill.

Place the brie, on the aluminum foil, on the side of the grill without the heat.

Grill the brie, lid closed, with indirect heat for 6–8 minutes or until the cheese is warm and soft. Watch closely to prevent the cheese from melting.

Serve with crackers.

BRINED, RUBBED, & CHERRY-SMOKED WINGS

16 whole chicken wings

4 cups (1 L) Poultry Brine (see page 233)

Canola oil (for brushing)

¼ cup (60 mL) brown sugar

2 tsp (10 mL) lemon pepper

1 tsp (5 mL) garlic powder

1 tsp (5 mL) dried rosemary leaves, crumbled

¼ tsp (1 mL) celery salt

¼ tsp (1 mL) seasoned salt

RINSE THE CHICKEN wings and pat them dry with paper towels. Remove and discard the wing tips.

Pour the 4 cups (1 L) poultry brine over the wings in a non-metallic, sealed container. Refrigerate for 12 hours.

Remove the wings from the brine, rinse under cold water, and pat dry with paper towels.

Place the wings in a large bowl and brush lightly with canola oil.

In a bowl, combine the remaining ingredients to create a brown sugar rub.

Sprinkle the brown sugar rub generously over the wings. Refrigerate for 15–30 minutes.

Set the smoker to medium (250°F/120°C) using cherry wood. Cook the wings for 2½ hours, turning every hour.

Winter, Wild and Wonderful

THE WARM OCTOBER weather we were enjoying while in Edmonton, Alberta, for a television interview suddenly turned cold and snowy. With another interview looming in Calgary, we had no choice but to undertake the treacherous drive south on Highway 2. We had to remove a layer of ice from the roof of the slide-out room on our 40-foot (12 meter) motor home. If the slide-out did not slide in, we were not going anywhere. Chipping the ice with a screwdriver was futile; a hair dryer on an extension cord got the job done.

Highway 2 south to Calgary was a rough, rugged, 192-mile (310 kilometer) ice rink. We crept the entire distance, emergency lights flashing, never touching the brakes. Fingers locked on the steering wheel, eyes peering ahead, we passed 60 vehicles in the ditch. We wished for a Chinook. The warm, dry wind of the Canadian Prairies and Great Plains can suddenly lift freezing temperatures to 65°F (18°C) in only a few hours and almost melt a foot of snow in a day.

We did not experience a Chinook, but when we left Calgary and turned west to the Rockies, dry pavement rolled once more beneath our wheels. Fresh snow covered distant slopes, outlining every tree. Distinctive mountain shapes, like the triple peaks of the Three Sisters near Canmore, stood out like a postcard in the clear, crisp air. The same snowy conditions that had made our trip from Edmonton to Calgary so treacherous had turned the Rocky Mountains into winter works of art.

SMOKEY SPICY SQUASH BISQUE

1 whole head of garlic, unpeeled

1 butternut squash, cut in half lengthwise, seeds removed

½ tsp (2 mL) salt

½ tsp (2 mL) pepper

½ chipotle pepper in adobo sauce

2 tsp (10 mL) butter

2 tsp (10 mL) extra-virgin olive oil + extra (for brushing)

½ cup (125 mL) finely chopped onion

¼ cup (60 mL) finely chopped celery

¼ cup (60 mL) finely chopped carrot

2 cups (500 mL) chicken stock

2 tsp (10 mL) chopped fresh cilantro

¾ cup (185 mL) 18% MF table cream

SLICE THE TOP off the head of garlic to expose the tip of the garlic cloves. Brush the outside skin of the garlic generously with olive oil.

Cut each half of the butternut squash into slices, widthwise, about 2 inches (5 cm) wide. Brush the flesh of the squash generously with olive oil and sprinkle with ½ tsp (2 mL) salt and ½ tsp (2 mL) pepper.

Preheat the smoker to medium-high (300°F/150°C), lid closed.

Cook the garlic, cut side up, for 1 hour. Cook the squash for 2 hours. Turn squash over halfway through the cooking time.

Transfer the garlic and squash from the smoker to a cutting board. When the squash is cool enough to touch, remove and discard the skin. Cut the flesh into 1-inch (2.5 cm) cubes.

Squeeze the flesh out of the garlic skin. Discard the skin. Finely chop the flesh.

Remove the seeds and membrane from the chipotle pepper and finely chop the pepper.

Heat the butter and olive oil in a large saucepan over medium heat. Add the onion, celery, carrot, and chipotle pepper. Stir and cook for 4 minutes.

Add the cut-up squash, garlic, and chicken stock to the pot. Stir. Bring to a boil, reduce the heat, and partially cover. Cook for 20 minutes, or until the vegetables are soft, stirring occasionally.

Turn off the heat. Stir in the cilantro and cream.

Puree the soup with a hand blender or food processor. Serve hot or chilled.

BURGERS, SANDWICHES, & PIZZA

Just a Mist of Whiskey, Please

LYNCHBURG, TENNESSEE, IS home to the Jack Daniel Distillery. Since 1866, every ounce of Jack Daniel's Tennessee Whiskey produced has come from the clear limestone spring water of this small southern town. At one time, the distillery bottled water as well. When it was discovered that there was more money in whiskey, the company stopped bottling water.

And at the end of each month, every Jack Daniel's employee receives a pint of whiskey. We were told that everyone shows up for work that day. In small-town fashion, employees celebrate Jack Daniel's birthday. His birthday was in September but because the employees at the distillery don't know exactly what day his birthday was, they celebrate it all month long.

Because Lynchburg is in a dry county, alcohol is not for purchase any day of the week, which is why we were served lemonade at the end of the distillery tour, not whiskey.

There is a small café across a footbridge from the Jack Daniel Distillery. On the menu, there are burgers with a choice of slaw, cheese, or a misting of whiskey. We asked how it was possible in a dry county to have whiskey on a burger. Our waitress explained that it was legal if it was just a light misting for cooking purposes. The whiskey-misted burger patty is their best seller.

The flavor was so good that we added it to our barbecue sauce.

WHISKEY BURGER WITH COLESLAW

¼ cup (60 mL) mayonnaise

½ tsp (2 mL) white sugar

Pinch of salt

Pinch of pepper

2 cups (500 mL) finely grated or chopped cabbage

2 Tbsp (30 mL) Tennessee sour mash whiskey

¼ cup (60 mL) barbecue sauce

Four ¼ lb (125 g) ground beef patties

4 hamburger buns

IN A SMALL bowl, combine the mayonnaise, sugar, salt, and pepper.

Place the cabbage in a bowl. Add the mayonnaise mixture. Mix well. Set the coleslaw aside.

In a small bowl, combine the whiskey and the barbecue sauce. Set aside.

Preheat the grill on high (550–600°F/290–315°C) for 10 minutes with the lid closed. Using a pair of long-handled tongs, oil the grate by wiping it with a piece of folded paper towel dipped lightly in canola oil. Reduce the heat to medium-high (450–550°F/230–290°C).

Grill the patties for 5 minutes with the lid closed. Turn the meat over and brush with the whiskey sauce. Grill for about 5 minutes on the second side or until the internal temperature registers 160°F (71°C) on an instant-read thermometer.

During the last minute of grilling time, place the hamburger buns cut-side down on the grate until they are a golden brown.

Transfer the cooked patties to a platter and brush both sides generously with the whiskey sauce. Put a hamburger patty on the bottom of each bun. Top each patty with the coleslaw.

Crazy for Veggies

DAILY SUNSHINE AND warm temperatures from November to March entice North Americans living in colder climates to become Winter Yumans. In addition to the good weather, Yuma, Arizona, has a lot of history. Museums tell stories of Yuma's unique past. The Yuma Quartermaster Depot supplied forts in five states, by mule train. The Yuma Territorial Prison, known as the "Country Club on the Colorado," incarcerated both men and women. The Yuma Landing Restaurant sits on the spot where the first airplane, rented from the Wright Brothers, landed in 1911. Casa de la Coronado displays artifacts and furniture from one of the first Best Western facilities in the country. An airplane hangs in the lobby of City Hall; in 1949, it was fueled from a convertible driving 80 miles (129 kilometers) an hour beneath it, enabling it to fly over 1,000 hours non-stop.

The sunshine, soil, and water of Yuma nurture over 175 different crops. Truckloads of fresh produce pass through cooling plants to reduce their temperatures before hitting the highways to grocery stores. Crops harvested in the morning can be in Phoenix by the afternoon and on the east coast of the United States in three to four days. Ninety percent of leafy vegetables produced in the United States in the winter months are grown in Yuma. Ancient Colorado River deposits created fields that are laser-leveled to generate two million pounds of bagged lettuce and salad mix every day.

MAKES 4 SERVINGS

SOUTHWEST VEGGIE BURGER

1 small zucchini

4 large white mushrooms

1 sweet onion

1 small sweet potato

1 small eggplant

1 red bell pepper

Canola oil (for brushing)

4 slices Monterey Jack cheese

4 large hamburger buns

1 cup (250 mL) Southwest salsa (see page 232)

CUT THE ZUCCHINI lengthwise into ¼-inch (6 mm) thick slices.

Cut the mushrooms lengthwise through the stems, into ¼-inch (6 mm) thick slices.

Cut the onion, sweet potato, and eggplant into ¼-inch (6 mm) thick rounds.

Cut the pepper into quarters, remove seeds, membrane, and stem.

Brush the vegetables on all sides with canola oil.

Slice hamburger buns and lightly brush both cut sides with canola oil.

Place a grill topper or griddle on one half of the grate.

Preheat the grill on high (550–600°F/290–315°C) for 10 minutes with the lid closed. Using a pair of long-handled tongs, oil the grate and the grill topper by wiping them with a piece of folded paper towel dipped lightly in canola oil.

Reduce the heat to medium (350–450°F/175–230°C).

Place the zucchini, mushroom, onion, and sweet potato slices on the grill topper. Place the pepper and eggplant directly on the grate.

Grill for about 4 minutes on each side. Remove individual vegetables as they become tender and slightly charred on both sides.

Place hamburger buns, cut side down, on the grate until lightly toasted.

Stack the grilled vegetables on the toasted buns. Top with Monterey Jack cheese slices. Serve with Southwest salsa.

PINEAPPLE PORK BURGER

2 Tbsp (30 mL) molasses

2 Tbsp (30 mL) ketchup

2 tsp (10 mL) Worcestershire sauce

½ tsp (2 mL) Dijon mustard

1 lb (450 g) ground pork

4 pineapple rings

4 hamburger buns

IN A SMALL bowl combine the molasses, ketchup, Worcestershire sauce, and mustard. Whisk the ingredients together.

Place the pork in a large mixing bowl. Add the molasses mixture to the ground pork. Mix well. Form the pork into 4 patties about ½ inch (1 cm) thick.

Preheat the grill on high (550–600°F/290–315°C) for 10 minutes with the lid closed. Using a pair of long-handled tongs, oil the grate by wiping it with a piece of folded paper towel dipped lightly in canola oil. Turn the heat to medium-high (450–550°F/230–290°C).

Grill the patties for about 5 minutes on each side with the lid closed, or until the internal temperature registers 160°F (71°C) on an instant-read thermometer. During the last 3 minutes of cooking time, place the pineapple rings on the grate to heat through and place the sliced hamburger buns face down on the grate to toast.

Serve the burgers with the pineapple rings on top of the meat.

AVOCADO TURKEY BURGER

1 egg white

¼ cup (60 mL) finely diced red
bell pepper

2 Tbsp (30 mL) finely chopped onion

1 garlic clove, finely chopped

½ tsp (2 mL) curry powder

½ tsp (2 mL) ground ginger

¼ cup (60 mL) breadcrumbs

1 lb (450 g) ground turkey

4 hamburger buns

Olive oil (for brushing)

1 ripe avocado

1 Tbsp (15 mL) lemon juice

1 tsp (5 mL) seasoned salt

IN A LARGE bowl, lightly whisk the egg white. Add the red pepper, onion, garlic, curry powder, ground ginger, and breadcrumbs. Mix the ingredients together.

Add the turkey to the bowl. Mix well. Form into 4 burger patties about ½ inch (1 cm) thick.

Preheat the grill on medium-high (450–550°F/230–290°C) for 10 minutes with the lid closed. Using a pair of long-handled tongs, oil the grate by wiping it with a piece of folded paper towel dipped lightly in canola oil. Reduce the heat to medium (350–450°F/175–230°C).

With the lid closed, grill the turkey burgers for 8–10 minutes on each side or until the internal temperature registers 180–185°F (82–85°C) on an instant-read thermometer inserted from the side into the center of the burger.

Brush the cut side of the buns with olive oil and toast them, cut side down, on the grate during the last minute of cooking time.

Peel the avocado and remove the pit. In a bowl, mash the avocado with a fork. Add the lemon juice and seasoned salt. Mix well.

Spread the mixture on the bottom half of each bun. Place the turkey patties on top of the avocado mixture.

Smorgasbord of Flavors

SOLVANG IS A small town in California's Santa Barbara wine country that began as a Danish settlement in the 1900s. Today, people travel there to experience the unique architecture, appreciate its history, and indulge in the Danish lifestyle. In the five-block downtown core there are five Danish bakeries. At sunrise, the sweet aroma of just-out-of-the-oven pastries and breads fills the early-morning air.

Choosing a pastry when there are so many available is not easy. Strudel. Butter cookies. Danishes. Tarts. Éclairs. We soon learned that the famous butter ring, an 8-inch (20 cm) round coffee cake made with real butter, almond paste, and custard at Mortensen's Bakery, sells out by early afternoon.

Ingeborg's Danish Chocolates continues to create chocolate exactly the way she made them in 1962. At Bacon & Brine, daily specials showcase pork and fermented greens.

The house specialty at the Greenhouse Café, a Nordic bistro, is *smorrebrod,* or Danish open-faced sandwiches.

At the Solvang Restaurant, we rolled up our sleeves and donned aprons to make *aebleskiver* by dropping pancake batter into circular holes in a copper griddle pan. These pancake balls are served with a dollop of raspberry jam and powdered sugar.

The original Danish smorgasbord was a variety of small select appetizers. The smorgasbord of flavors offered by Solvang's restaurants and bakeries is immense.

Solvang's '50s-style diner, Chomps, serves a Caprese burger stacked with large fragrant basil leaves and mozzarella cheese. Like Chomps, we took the primary ingredients of a Caprese salad and creatively added them to a burger (see next page).

BASIL BALSAMIC BAGEL BURGER

10 sun-dried tomatoes

1 garlic clove, peeled and cut in half

¼ cup (60 mL) balsamic vinegar

½ cup (125 mL) extra-virgin olive oil + extra (for brushing)

Four ¼-lb (125 g) ground beef patties

4 plain or multi-grain bagels

12 large fresh basil leaves

4 tomato slices

4 thick slices fresh mozzarella

PLACE THE SUN-DRIED tomatoes in a bowl and cover with boiling water. Set aside. After 5 minutes, drain the tomatoes and discard the water.

Place the sun-dried tomatoes and garlic in a food processor and process until the pieces are small.

Add the balsamic vinegar and olive oil. Blend until the mixture is smooth. Set aside.

Preheat the grill on high (550–600°F/290–315°C) for 10 minutes with the lid closed. Using a pair of long-handled tongs, oil the grate by wiping it with a piece of folded paper towel dipped lightly in canola oil.

Grill the ground beef patties about 5 minutes on each side or until the internal temperature registers 160°F (71°C) on an instant-read thermometer.

While the patties are cooking, cut the bagels in half and brush each cut side with olive oil.

Toast the bagel halves cut-side down on the grate until golden brown, about 2 minutes.

Place the toasted bagel halves open-faced on serving plates.

Spread all 8 bagel halves generously with the sun-dried tomato mixture.

Place 3 basil leaves on the bottom half of each bagel. Place the cooked beef patty on top of the basil. Follow with the tomato and mozzarella.

Refrigerate leftover sun-dried tomato mixture in a covered container for up to 1 week.

US Highway 2 is Not a Freeway

A FREEWAY GETS us to our destination quickly, but we prefer to experience the amazing geographic and cultural differences that are found only in rural areas and small towns, which is why we took US Highway 2 from Upper Michigan to Washington State.

As we began our journey, grass-covered sand dunes and small whitecaps followed us along the north shore of Lake Michigan. When the road dipped into Wisconsin, and then returned to Michigan's Upper Peninsula briefly before settling back into Wisconsin, we stopped to sample Cornish pasties, wild rice, and frozen custard. In Ashland, murals on downtown buildings display the importance of timber to the history of the town. A huge statue of Paul Bunyan and his Blue Ox, Babe, overlook the shore of Lake Bemidji where it is said he returns annually to fish.

Rugby, North Dakota, is the geographic center of North America. It was in Rugby we met a local rancher who, implying that the little smart car hitched behind our RV was an insect, said "We have spray for that."

When we crossed into Montana, red gravel side roads disappeared over distant hills with barely a tree in sight. In Culbertson, we discovered we were in Lewis and Clark territory. On the outskirts of Saco, Montana, white pelicans amused themselves in a marshy pond. Farther down the road, Dodson, Montana, is almost a ghost town. A faded billboard promoting a casino suggested "Gambling is definitely more fun than feeding cows."

Near Spokane, Washington, logging trucks outnumbered cars on the road. Leavenworth, Washington, is like an Alpine village set amongst tall evergreen trees, a frothy white river, and the mountains of the Wenatchee National Forest.

Driving from Michigan to Washington by freeway would have been quite different.

OPEN-FACED STEAK BRUSCHETTA SANDWICH

1 cup (250 mL) quartered cherry tomatoes

3 Tbsp (45 mL) pitted, chopped kalamata olives

1 Tbsp (15 mL) finely chopped red onion

2 tsp (10 mL) finely chopped fresh basil

2 tsp (10 mL) white balsamic vinegar

1 Tbsp (15 mL) extra-virgin olive oil

Two 1-lb (450 g) boneless blade steaks

½ tsp (2 mL) sea salt

½ tsp (2 mL) coarsely ground pepper

1 Italian baguette, cut into 4 pieces

2 Tbsp (30 mL) melted butter

2–3 cups (500–750 mL) baby salad greens

IN A BOWL, combine tomatoes, olives, onion, basil, vinegar, and olive oil. Set aside.

Sprinkle steaks with salt and pepper.

Preheat the grill on high (550–600°F/290–315°C) for 10 minutes with the lid closed. Using a pair of long-handled tongs, oil the grate by wiping it with a piece of folded paper towel dipped lightly in canola oil.

Reduce the heat to medium-high (450–550°F/230–290°C). Place steaks on the grate and cook with the lid closed for 5–6 minutes per side or until the internal temperature registers 135°F (57°C) for medium-rare on an instant-read thermometer.

Transfer the steaks to a cutting board. Do not turn off the grill.

Let the steaks rest for 10 minutes before slicing thinly against the grain.

Slice each section of the baguette in half lengthwise. Brush the cut sides with the melted butter. Place cut sides down on the grate until browned, about 2–3 minutes.

To assemble, place the steak slices on the bread and top with baby greens and the tomato mixture.

Wit or Wit-Out Cheese in South Philly

IN ORDER TO experience real Philly cheesesteak we went to the source, Philadelphia, Pennsylvania, or South Philly, to be precise. Two cheesesteak purveyors compete at the intersection of 9th Street and Passyunk Avenue. Pat's King of Steaks is said to be the originator of the steak sandwich. In 1933, Pat Olivieri and his brother Harry were operating a hot dog stand. Tired of hot dogs, they grilled thinly cut, inexpensive steak and ate it on a roll with grilled onions. After sampling the chopped steak, a cabbie suggested they forget about the hot dogs. In 1966, Joey Vento opened his doors across the street. His son Geno, of Geno's Steaks, admits his family didn't invent the sandwich but just perfected it.

A bona fide Philly cheesesteak is served on a long, soft, slightly salted roll. In Philadelphia, rolls from only two baking companies, Amoroso's and Vilotti-Pisanelli, are acceptable to die-hard steak sandwich enthusiasts. Thinly sliced rib eye steak is grilled, placed on the roll, and topped with grilled onions and cheese. The choices in cheese are provolone, American, Cheez Whiz, and at Pat's location, mozzarella as well.

Caught up in the competition between the two companies we decided to sample from both Pat's and Geno's. Geno's caught our attention first. It is hard to miss. We stepped up to the take-out window under the bright lights, shiny orange canopy, and stainless steel of their 24-hour operation to order "provolone with" and "Whiz with." Every bite transported us to cheesesteak nirvana. The roll was soft but firm, the meat was tender, the onions caramelized, and the cheese melted. At Pat's, we stepped up to the less glamorous take-out window of a typical fast food stand. We each ordered again, this time using our newly acquired South Philly lingo. "Whiz wit" and "Whiz wit-out."

Geno and Pat both make great Philly cheesesteaks. So do we (see next page).

PHILLY CHEESESTEAK

4 soft hoagie rolls
(7–8 inches/18–20 cm long)

3 Tbsp (45 mL) canola oil

3 medium-sized onions, peeled, sliced
into thin rings

2 lb (900 g) very thinly sliced,
rib eye steak

Pinch of salt

Pinch of pepper

8 slices provolone cheese or ½ cup
(125 mL) Cheese Whiz

PLACE A GRIDDLE on the grill grate. Preheat the grill on medium-high (450–550°F/230–290°C) for 10 minutes with the lid closed.

Slice the buns open lengthwise and place on individual plates. Set aside.

Pour the oil onto the griddle and spread over the surface. Add the onions. Stir and cook until they are tender, approximately 3–4 minutes. Transfer the onions to a plate. Set aside.

Place the steak on the griddle and cook until lightly browned, approximately 3–4 minutes. Sprinkle with salt and pepper. Add extra oil to the griddle, if necessary.

Divide the meat into 8 portions on the griddle. Place the onions on top of each portion of the meat. Place slices of provolone cheese or spoon Cheese Whiz on top of the onions. Close the lid.

When the cheese has melted, transfer the meat portions to the 4 buns, 2 portions per bun.

A Sandwich by Any Other Name

MOST NORTH AMERICANS know that a submarine sandwich consists of a long roll filled with a choice of meats, cheeses, vegetables, seasonings, and sauces. However, as we travel, we discover that the big sandwich is not necessarily called a submarine. In New York City, a similar sandwich is a hero. North of New York City, perhaps because the bread is cut on the diagonal or because the fillings are squeezed so tightly into position, the staple of the lunch break is known as a wedge. Philadelphia calls it a hoagie. A type of submarine sandwich in New Orleans is served on a baguette and called a po' boy. At a restaurant in New England, we ordered a grinder.

Sometimes, sandwich nomenclature refers to the shape of the bread. Torpedo, bomber, blimpie, gondola, or zep (as in zeppelin). Justifiably so, these names create images of huge sandwiches for people with extraordinary appetites.

There are many explanations as to how these variations on the submarine came about. Most make reference to Italian immigration to North America after the First World War. At that time, salami, beef, and sausage were the most popular meats. Lettuce, tomato, oil, and vinegar were the accompaniments. Today, restaurants are likely to offer non-traditional ingredients that reflect the ethnicity and natural bounty of the area or the chef's individual creativity. The 18th-century Earl of Sandwich—where the sandwich got its name—would be impressed.

One of our favorites is the spiedie (see next page), a sandwich originating in Binghamton, New York, with cubed meat that has been marinated and grilled. Traditionally the skewer of meat is inserted inside a thick slice of Italian bread. The bread is used to grip the meat and pull it off the skewer to make the sandwich.

CHICKEN SPIEDIE

¾ cup (185 mL) extra-virgin olive oil

¼ cup (60 mL) balsamic vinegar

½ cup (125 mL) white vinegar

2 Tbsp (30 mL) white sugar

1 small onion, coarsely chopped

4 cloves garlic, thinly sliced

½ tsp (2 mL) salt

½ tsp (2 mL) pepper

1 tsp (5 mL) dried thyme leaves

1 tsp (5 mL) dried marjoram leaves

1 tsp (5 mL) dried oregano leaves

Four 6–8 oz (170–230 g) boneless, skinless chicken breasts

4–6 thick slices of Italian bread or long, soft rolls

IN A BOWL, combine the olive oil, vinegars, sugar, onion, garlic, salt, pepper, thyme, marjoram, and oregano. Mix well.

Cut the chicken breasts into approximately 1-inch (2.5 cm) cubes.

Pour the marinade into a resealable plastic bag and add the chicken cubes. Seal tightly and shake to coat the chicken. Place the bag flat on a plate in the refrigerator and marinate for 12–24 hours. Discard the marinade.

If using wooden, not metal skewers, soak in water for 30 minutes before using.

Thread the chicken cubes onto metal or wooden skewers with space between the pieces to ensure the chicken cooks evenly.

Preheat the grill on medium (350–450°F/175–230°C) for 10 minutes with the lid closed. Using a pair of long-handled tongs, oil the grate by wiping it with a piece of folded paper towel dipped lightly in canola oil.

Cook the chicken with the lid closed for 4–6 minutes on each side or until the chicken is cooked through.

Remove chicken from the skewers and place on slices of bread or in a long, soft roll.

Experiencing San Benito County

THERE ARE TWO towns in San Benito County, California. Hollister has all the amenities of a modern city while historic San Juan Bautista surrounds the Mission San Juan Bautista, the largest church on the California Mission Trail.

In San Juan Bautista, the San Juan Bakery heats up a 1938 brick oven with a torch and their sourdough starter dates back to the 1820s. Dona Esther, voted the best Mexican restaurant in the county, serves outstanding Nachos Supreme. In Hollister, Mansmith's food truck serves up mouth-watering barbecue and award-winning sauces and spices. Casa de Fruta, a California landmark, is the place to go for fruit, vegetables, fruit wines, candy, or a meal, all within a family-oriented Disney-type setting. Paine's Restaurant was the first to bring lightly breaded, tender calamari to Hollister menus. At B&R Farms, the owners work hard to protect and produce the precious Blenheim apricot. At Benito Bene, hand-crafted and natural products are produced by local artisans. The Joshua Inn Bed & Breakfast combines southern hospitality with a good breakfast experience that includes juice from oranges that grow in the backyard. At Suncoast Organic Farm, organic grains are ground into flour for artisanal breads and pastries, all baked in a wood-fired oven in their bakery. The Inn at Tres Pinos offers upscale continental cuisine in a rustic building that was once a stagecoach stop and brothel.

At the end of each day of our tasting tour of San Benito County, we returned to the RV at the Bolado Park Event Center, surrounded by country charm and old oak trees. Pinnacles National Park was just down the road.

SMOKE & SALAD GOURMET BURGER

Four 4-oz (110 g) ground beef patties

2 tsp (10 mL) balsamic vinegar

1 Tbsp (15 mL) extra-virgin olive oil
+ extra (for brushing)

2 cups (500 mL) fresh arugula

4 large pretzel buns

2 Tbsp (30 mL) melted butter

4–6 Tbsp (60–90 mL) Smoked Garlic Aioli (see page 231)

16 Smoker-Roasted Caramelized Tomatoes (see page 211)

PREHEAT THE SMOKER to high (375–400°F/190–200°C).

Make a wide, shallow indent in the center of each patty to prevent puffing up in the middle.

Lightly brush both sides of the patties with olive oil. Place the beef patties on the grate, indent-side down. Cook for 10–15 minutes on each side or until the internal temperature registers 160°F (71°C) on an instant-read thermometer.

In a bowl, whisk the vinegar and oil together. Add the arugula and toss lightly.

To warm the buns, brush the cut sides with the butter and place cut-side down on the smoker for about 5 minutes.

Spread a layer of Smoked Garlic Aioli on the inside bottom of each pretzel bun.

Top with Smoker-Roasted Tomato Slices, beef patties, and a pile of the arugula.

Any Road Will Take You There

SOMETIMES ON THE road we expect to find one thing and end up experiencing something completely different. This is what happened when we drove into Kosciusko, Mississippi. We went there because it was Oprah Winfrey's birthplace. At the Visitor Center, we asked advice on what to see while in Kosciusko. In addition to the church that Oprah attended as a little girl, they suggested we visit the home of the artist L.V. Hull.

We parked the car in front of L.V. Hull's tiny house. Her front yard was filled with television sets, shoes, purses, plastic ducks, mailboxes, egg cartons, hard hats, old telephones, and tires, all of them painted in bright colors and accented with polka dots. There might have been a lawn mower in there somewhere. If so, it was painted too.

"I am an artist. I do the L.V. to whatever people bring me," she said.

L.V. beckoned to us from her oversized chair just inside her open front door. Her living room overflowed with dotted things. So did her bedroom, kitchen, and bathroom. Along a narrow path through the middle of her living room, we discovered a pile of ceiling-fan blades. Each fan blade was painted with polka dots and a message. We bought the one that said, "If you don't know where you are going, any road will take you there." Very appropriate for people always looking for new adventure.

A quote from Oprah is on display at the Visitor Center: "When ordinary people decide to do extraordinary things, they transform their own lives and the lives of those around them." In her own unique way, L.V. Hull has done just that.

SMOKED BACON BURGER DOG

1 lb (450 g) lean ground beef

1 chipotle pepper in adobo sauce

1 tsp (5 mL) garlic powder

¼ tsp (1 mL) pepper

7 heaping tsp (approx. 35 mL) shredded mozzarella cheese

7 wieners

7 strips of thinly sliced bacon

7 hot dog buns

PLACE THE GROUND beef in a bowl. Remove the seeds and membrane from the chipotle pepper. (If the seeds and the membrane are not removed, the heat of the pepper could be intolerable.) Chop the pepper and add it to the ground beef bowl. Mix in the garlic powder and pepper.

Divide the meat mixture into 7 equal balls. Place 1 ball on a cutting board and flatten it into the shape of a hamburger patty about ¼-inch (6 mm) thick.

Sprinkle 1 heaping tsp (approx. 5 mL) mozzarella over the meat.

Place a wiener on the front edge of the meat and roll the meat around the wiener. Press the meat onto the wiener to seal the edges.

Wrap a thin strip of bacon diagonally from one end of the wiener to the other, leaving spaces between each wrap so the bacon reaches end to end. Repeat with the remaining meatballs and wieners.

Preheat the smoker to high (350°F/175°C). Place the bacon burger dogs on the grate and cook for about 40 minutes. Turn and rotate the bacon burger dogs after 20 minutes. Serve in a large hot dog bun with all the trimmings.

La Plume est Morte

WHEN WE TELL people that we went to France, just a 55-minute ferry ride from Canada, we often get a look of disbelief. Saint-Pierre and Miquelon, French territorial islands off the south coast of Newfoundland and Labrador, are almost 3,000 miles (4,830 kilometers) from France but less than 20 miles (32 kilometers) from Canada's most easterly province.

From the moment we docked on Saint-Pierre, the larger of the two inhabited islands, the atmosphere reminded us of Europe. People sat at outdoor cafes with coffee and fresh pastries. Small European cars curved their way along narrow streets. In the main square, across from the ferry terminal, adults lounged on park benches. Several children stood in line for a ride on a carousel, others were eating ice cream cones. We wanted ice cream, too, but as we joined the line, we realized that euros were required. We hadn't exchanged our dollars before leaving the mainland.

The friendly people at the tourism office directed us to a bank. When we decided to stay overnight, they helped us with that too. Our bed and breakfast host was 81-year-old Madame Vigneau, who spoke very little English. Her home was immaculate and her breakfast exquisite with croissants, jams, and coffee. We thanked her in our best high-school French. When her pen went dry while we were signing her guest book, we had to tell her that her pen had died, "la plume est morte," because we did not know the French words for "ran out of ink."

The 10-square-mile (16 kilometer) island of Saint-Pierre enjoys wine, bread, coffee, fashions, and automobiles from France with fresh produce from Canada. The best of the new and old world.

SKEWERED SMOKEY MEATBALL BAGUETTE

2 large eggs

½ cup (125 mL) dry breadcrumbs

3 Tbsp (45 mL) finely grated
Parmesan cheese

2 Tbsp (30 mL) fresh chives,
finely chopped

2 cloves garlic, finely chopped

¼ tsp (1 mL) salt

½ tsp (2 mL) pepper

1 lb (450 g) ground beef

½ lb (225 g) ground pork

1–2 Tbsp (15–30 mL) canola oil
(for brushing)

2 French baguettes
(about 20 inches/50 cm long)

1–1¼ cups (250–310 mL) shredded
mozzarella cheese

1½–2 cup (375–500 mL)
storebought marinara sauce

SOAK 5 LONG wooden skewers in water for 30 minutes.

In a large bowl, whisk the eggs. Stir in the breadcrumbs, Parmesan, chives, garlic, salt, and pepper. Mix well.

In a separate bowl, combine the ground beef and the ground pork. Add this to the egg mixture and mix together.

Shape the meat into 20 golf ball–sized meatballs. Put 4 meatballs on each skewer with space between each meatball. Brush the canola oil over the surface of the meatballs.

Preheat the smoker to medium-high (325°F/160°C). Place the skewered meatballs on the grate. Cook the meatballs for about 30 minutes or until the meatball centers reach 165°F (74°C) on an instant-read thermometer.

While the meatballs are cooking, cut each baguette into 3 equal lengths. Slice each baguette lengthwise along the side but not all the way through. Scoop out a little of the bread to create space for the meatballs.

Sprinkle shredded mozzarella cheese on both inside halves of each baguette. Toast baguettes in a toaster oven or under a broiler to melt the cheese.

Heat the marinara sauce in a saucepan until hot and bubbly. Slide the meatballs off the skewers into the baguettes on top of the cheese. Spoon hot marinara sauce over the meatballs.

At the End of the Silver Trail

WE FOUND ONE of the best pizzas ever in Keno City, located in the mountains at the end of the Silver Trail in Canada's Yukon Territory, total population 12–25 people. Once one of the most productive mining areas in the country, Keno City now consists of a mining museum, a snack bar, several artists, and a few old-timers who stayed on after the mine shut down.

On a wet, muddy day, after touring the museum that was once the dance hall, movie theater, and community meeting place for miners and their families, we stopped at the Keno City Snack Bar. The owner talked about his parents who arrived from Italy to work hard on the Silver Trail. The homemade pizza on his menu was his mother's recipe.

As we were leaving the café, an older gentleman approached us with two small bouquets of wildflowers he had just picked in the drizzling rain. His gesture touched us deeply. As we drove away, down the long, lonely road out of Keno City, words describing our vagabond life spilled onto paper in the form of this poem.

> We drive into people's lives
> Share the hour
> And drive out again
> Wondering
> If we will ever see them again
> And, if we stayed longer
> Would the withdrawal be as intense
> Would the sweetness be diluted
> We meet by chance
> Connecting
> At a moment in time
> At a particular place on earth
> We leave
> Glad to have been there
> Because after all
> For that moment in time
> It was our favorite place on earth

What better way to celebrate our Keno City experience than with a pizza recipe inspired by the visit (see next page).

SUN-DRIED TOMATO & ARTICHOKE PIZZA

6 sun-dried tomatoes in oil, drained

6 oz (170 g) jar marinated artichoke hearts, drained

½ cup (125 mL) sliced, pitted kalamata olives

½ tsp (2 mL) anise seeds

1 cup (250 mL) shredded mozzarella cheese

⅓ portion Basic Grilling Pizza Dough (see page 234)

Olive oil

1½ Tbsp (23 mL) coarsely chopped fresh parsley

CUT THE SUN-DRIED tomatoes into small pieces. Trim any tough pieces from the artichoke hearts and cut the hearts into quarters. Portion out the olives, anise, and mozzarella by placing each pizza topping in a separate bowl. Set aside.

Generously brush a 16 × 11-inch (40 × 28 cm) cookie sheet with olive oil. Stretch the dough to an even thickness on the cookie sheet. Let the dough rest once or twice so it can relax before further stretching. The dough doesn't need to be perfectly square or round.

Lightly brush the top of the dough with olive oil.

Preheat the grill on medium-high (450–550°F/230–290°C) for 10 minutes with the lid closed. Using a pair of long-handled tongs, oil the grate by wiping it with a piece of folded paper towel dipped lightly in canola oil. Turn one side of the grill to medium (350–450°F/175–230°C). Turn the other side to low.

With hands or a large lifter, begin by lifting one end of the pizza crust from the cookie sheet. Slide the crust off the cookie sheet onto the hot side of the grill.

With the grill lid open, brown the bottom side for about 3 minutes or until the crust slides easily on the grate.

When the bottom side is well browned, turn the pizza crust over. Grill the second side of the crust on the hot side of the grill for about 2 minutes.

With tongs or a lifter, move the pizza crust to the cooler side of the grate.

Quickly spread the mozzarella over the surface of the crust. Sprinkle the sun-dried tomatoes, artichoke hearts, olives, and anise evenly over the cheese.

Close the grill lid. Grill for about 2 minutes or until the toppings are heated through and the cheese is melted.

Slide the hot pizza onto a cutting board. Sprinkle the pizza with the chopped parsley.

TIP For 4 servings, it is easier to manage 2 smaller pizzas on the grill rather than double the size of the crust.

Everybody is a Cook in Hoboken

ALONG A ROW of brownstone houses in Hoboken, New Jersey, neighborhood friends Helena, Rose, and Vinny were standing in their adjoining sandbox-sized front yards.

"Everybody is a cook in Hoboken," Rose said. "It used to be that every building, every family was Italian. We loved everybody here. When I went out into the world I wasn't afraid of anybody."

"They know how to cook here," Helena told us. "Years ago, a guy went up and down the street selling calves' liver. There was no refrigeration on his truck. I'd tell him not to open the truck, to just pass me the liver."

Helena, Rose, and Vinny live within a few doorsteps of Fiore's, the kind of deli all of us would like to have in our neighborhood. Every morning except Sunday, mozzarella is handmade in a back room using the recipe that has been handed down for generations.

Hoboken, New Jersey, the Mile Square City, looks across the Hudson River to lower Manhattan. The Statue of Liberty is just around the corner. Other than a city where, according to Rose, everyone is a cook, Hoboken is known as the birthplace of Frank Sinatra and the site of the first officially recorded baseball game.

Our Caprese pizza (see next page) recipe would score a home run with Fiore's fresh mozzarella.

CAPRESE PIZZA

⅓ portion Basic Grilling Pizza Dough (see page 234)

3 Tbsp (45 mL) grated Parmesan cheese

6–8 oz (170–230 g) sliced fresh mozzarella cheese

3–4 Roma tomatoes, thinly sliced

½ cup (125 mL) thin strips of fresh basil leaves

1 Tbsp (15 mL) extra-virgin olive oil

½ tsp (2 mL) garlic powder

¼ tsp (1 mL) sea salt

At least 1 Tbsp (15 mL) store-bought balsamic glaze

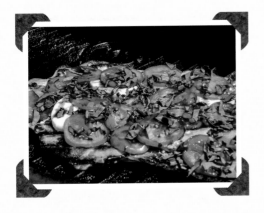

GENEROUSLY COAT A 16 × 11-inch (40 × 28 cm) cookie sheet with olive oil. Stretch the dough to an even thickness on the cookie sheet. Let it rest once or twice so the dough can relax before further stretching. The dough does not need to be perfectly square or round.

Place the Parmesan cheese, mozzarella cheese, tomatoes, and basil in separate dishes. Set aside.

In a small bowl, combine oil, garlic powder, and salt. Mix well.

Brush the top of the pizza dough with the olive oil and garlic mixture.

Preheat the grill on medium-high (450–550°F/230–290°C) for 10 minutes with the lid closed. Using a pair of long-handled tongs, oil the grate by wiping it with a piece of folded paper towel dipped lightly in canola oil. Turn one side of the grill to medium (350–450°F/175–230°C). Turn the other side to low (250–300°F/120–150°C).

With hands or a large lifter, begin by lifting one end of the pizza crust from the cookie sheet. Slide the crust off the cookie sheet onto the hot side of the grill.

With the grill lid open, brown the bottom side for about 3 minutes or until the crust slides easily on the grate.

When the bottom side is well browned, turn the pizza crust over. Grill the second side of the crust on the hot side of the grill for about 2 minutes.

With tongs or a lifter, move the pizza crust to the cooler side of the grate.

Quickly sprinkle the Parmesan over the crust. Place the mozzarella slices over the Parmesan. Arrange the tomato slices over the mozzarella.

Close the grill lid. Grill for about 2 minutes or until the toppings are heated through and the cheese has started to melt.

Slide the hot pizza onto a cutting board. Sprinkle the basil generously over top. Drizzle with balsamic glaze.

TIP For 4 servings, it is easier to manage 2 smaller pizzas on the grill rather than double the size of the crust.

PORK

Curtis's All American Bar-B-Q

WE WERE WINDING our way through mountains, photographing red barns and maple trees, when we stumbled upon Curtis in Putney, Vermont. In the small village nestled under Putney Mountain, the immediately identifiable aroma and blue smoke of barbecue caught our attention. We drove directly to the source—Curtis's All American Bar-B-Q—touted as the ninth wonder of the world. We were not expecting to see southern barbecue in a state so well known for maple syrup, cheddar cheese, and apples.

In earlier times, Curtis Tuff and his family worked their way north along the migrant trail in the eastern United States, picking the crops all the way from Florida to New York. A side step took them over to Vermont for the apple crops. When Curtis settled in the Putney area, he set up a roadside pit and cooked the food he loved.

Curtis's smoke pit is mounted on a trailer behind a bright blue, converted school bus with a take-out window. The lineups begin by the time the first flames of his morning fire reduce down to glowing coals. At one time Curtis' operation was mobile, traveling to different festivals and events. When we met him, the tires on his trailer no longer had treads: the rubber had long since melted in the heat of his hardwood fire.

Curtis works with a supervisor, Curtis Jr., who sleeps on the job, in a pen next to the barbecue pit. As the family pet—a white and black striped potbelly pig—Curtis Jr. dines on carrots.

With influences from his home state of Georgia, Curtis slathers his pork and chicken with a secret sauce that is sweet, tangy, and spicy.

APPLE RUM BACK RIBS

Two 1½-lb (700 g) racks pork
back ribs

3 cups (750 mL) sweet apple cider

¼ cup (60 mL) dark rum

½ tsp (2 mL) sea salt

½ tsp (2 mL) coarsely ground
pepper

PLACE THE RIBS in a large flat dish. Cut the racks in half to fit, if necessary. Combine the apple cider, rum, salt, and pepper. Pour the mixture over the ribs. Cover and marinate the ribs for 6–8 hours in the refrigerator. Turn the ribs over in the marinade once or twice.

Place a ceramic drip pan or foil half pan under the grate on one side of the grill.

Remove the ribs from the marinade and pour the marinade mixture into the drip pan.

Preheat the grill on low (250–300°F/120–150°C) on the drip pan side and on medium-high (450–550°F/230–290°C) on the other side for 10 minutes with the lid closed. Using a pair of long-handled tongs, oil the grate by wiping it with a piece of folded paper towel dipped lightly in canola oil.

Place the ribs on the grate over the drip pan. Close the grill lid.

After 30 minutes, turn the heat off under the drip pan. Turn the ribs over. If necessary add water to the drip pan to prevent it from going dry. Cook the ribs for 2 hours longer or until the meat is tender enough to pull the ribs apart and the ends of the bones are protruding. Rotate and turn the ribs every 30 minutes during the cooking time.

SMOKED ROSEMARY-BRINED PORK LOIN

2 cups (500 mL) apple juice

½ cup (125 mL) apple cider vinegar

½ cup (125 mL) water

1 Tbsp (15 mL) dried rosemary, crumbled

½ cup (125 mL) brown sugar

2 Tbsp (30 mL) sea salt

2–3 lb (0.9–1.4 kg) boneless pork loin roast

2 cups (500 mL) barbecue sauce (approx.)

IN A BOWL, combine the apple juice, vinegar, water, rosemary, brown sugar, and salt.

Put the pork in a resealable plastic bag. Pour the brine mixture over the pork. Seal the bag. Place the bag on a flat dish and set it in the refrigerator to marinate for 12–24 hours. Turn the bag over once or twice so every surface of the pork comes in contact with the brine.

Preheat the smoker to high (350°F/175°C).

Remove the pork loin from the brine and pat dry with paper towels. Discard the brine.

Place the pork roast, fat side up, on a rack in a shallow roasting pan.

Put the roasting pan on the smoker grate and roast for 2–2½ hours or until the roast registers 160°F (71°C) on an instant-read thermometer. Slather the pork with barbecue sauce every 30 minutes.

HICKORY-SMOKED EASTERN NORTH CAROLINA PULLED PORK

4–5 lb (1.8–2.2 kg) boneless pork
shoulder roast (Boston butt)

½ cup (125 mL) brown sugar

2 Tbsp (30 mL) dry mustard

2 tsp (10 mL) garlic powder

2 tsp (10 mL) pepper

2 tsp (10 mL) salt

1 tsp (5 mL) smoked paprika

3 cups (750 mL) Eastern North
Carolina Mopping Sauce
(see page 230), divided

PAT THE PORK roast dry with paper towels and place it in a large bowl or
flat dish.

In a bowl, combine the brown sugar, mustard, garlic powder, pepper,
salt, and paprika.

Generously rub the brown sugar mixture over the pork. Wrap the
pork in plastic wrap and refrigerate for 12–24 hours.

Using hickory wood, preheat the smoker to medium (250°F/120°C).

Set 1 cup (250 mL) of the Eastern North Carolina Mopping Sauce
aside. You'll use the remaining 2 cups (500 mL) of sauce over the pork as
it cooks.

Place the pork shoulder, fat-side down, on the grate and cook for
3 hours. Brush the pork with the mopping sauce every 30 minutes.

Turn the pork shoulder over and cook for another 3 hours, fat-side up.
Brush the pork with the mopping sauce every 30 minutes.

Remove the roast from the smoker and wrap in 2 layers of heavy-duty
foil, fat-side up.

Return the foil-wrapped roast to the 250°F (120°C) smoker for
another 2 hours or until the internal temperature registers 200°F (95°C)
on an instant-read thermometer.

Remove from the smoker and place the foil-wrapped roast in a roasting pan. Cover the pan with a lid or with foil. Let the wrapped roast rest
for 30 minutes in the covered roasting pan.

Carefully remove the foil surrounding the roast, allowing any juices
to run out of the foil and into the roasting pan with the pork. Cut and
remove any strings on the roast.

Pull the pork into chunks. Mix the reserved 1 cup (250 mL) mopping
sauce into the pulled pork.

Serve immediately, or cover the roasting pan and keep warm on the
grill or in an oven set at 200°F (95°C) for up to 1 hour.

B. B. King's Memphis Blues & Barbecue

AT GENUINE BARBECUE establishments, we often follow a trail of smoke in the parking lot to find a billowing smoker tucked away beside a pile of split wood. We check out barbecue pits in blackened kitchens. A sure sign of a good barbecue restaurant is the mixed aromas of smoke and sauce as we step inside the dining room door. We went to Memphis, Tennessee, to find good barbecue.

B.B. King's Blues Club in Memphis, Tennessee, is one of the ultimate barbecue experiences because it is a combination of southern food and B.B.'s music. Blown-up photos and paintings of B.B., Muddy Waters, Furry Lewis, Bob Dylan, and other musicians hang alongside several of the "Lucille" Gibson guitars that B.B. strummed to create his signature blues sound. Folk art covers the tabletops.

Drums and microphones are ready on a well-used stage for the next performance of blues, soul, pop, and classic rock.

B.B. loved the music of New Orleans and the Mississippi Delta. His supper club menu includes southern comfort appetizers and sides. You'll find fried dill pickles, catfish, black-eyed pea hummus, crawfish, fried green tomatoes, fire-cracked corn, collard greens, and cornbread. The ribs are the number-one selling entrée. Served with baked beans and coleslaw, they can be ordered wet or Memphis-style (dry with a side of sauce).

A Friday night in Memphis, listening to live southern soul and nibbling on southern-flavored Memphis-style dry ribs—what a great way to celebrate a blues musician's life.

SMOKED MEMPHIS-STYLE DRY RIBS

2 cups (500 mL) apple cider vinegar

¼ cup (60 mL) water

5 Tbsp (75 mL) Memphis-Style Dry Rub (see page 231), divided

2 Tbsp (30 mL) canola oil

Two 2½–3 lb (1.1–1.4 kg) racks of side or back ribs

At least 4 oz (110 g) barbecue sauce (optional)

IN A LARGE container, combine vinegar, water, 3 Tbsp (45 mL) Memphis-Style Dry Rub, and canola oil. Set aside.

Preheat the smoker to medium-high (325°F/160°C) using hickory wood.

Place the ribs on the grate and close the lid. Cook for about 2½ hours or until the meat is tender enough to pull the ribs apart and the ends of the bones are protruding. During cooking time, mop the ribs every 20 minutes with the vinegar mixture and turn the ribs over.

Transfer the ribs to a large platter and lightly mop one last time. Sprinkle the top of the ribs with the remaining dry rub.

Serve with barbecue sauce on the side (optional).

PORK LOIN CHERRIES JUBILEE

2 Tbsp (30 mL) red wine vinegar

3 Tbsp (45 mL) fresh lemon juice, divided

1 Tbsp (15 mL) Worcestershire sauce

1 tsp (5 mL) dry mustard

½ cup (125 mL) orange juice

1 small onion, thinly sliced

½ tsp (2 mL) pepper

2 lb (900 g) pork loin roast

¾ cup (185 mL) pitted sour cherries

½ cup (125 mL) cherry juice

½ Tbsp (7.5 mL) brown sugar

1 Tbsp (15 mL) cornstarch

2 Tbsp (30 mL) water

3 Tbsp (45 mL) brandy

IN A BOWL, combine the vinegar, 2 Tbsp (30 mL) lemon juice, Worcestershire sauce, dry mustard, orange juice, onion, and pepper. Mix the ingredients thoroughly and place them in a large resealable plastic bag.

Add the pork loin to the mixture. Seal the bag and refrigerate for 12–24 hours. Turn the bag over at least once while the pork marinates.

Remove the pork from the marinade. Discard the marinade.

Preheat the grill on medium-high (450–550°F/230–290°C) for 10 minutes with the lid closed. Using a pair of long-handled tongs, oil the grate by wiping it with a piece of folded paper towel dipped lightly in canola oil.

Sear the roast for about 4 minutes on each side with the lid closed.

Turn the heat off on the side of the grill beneath the pork. With the lid closed, cook and turn the roast every 15 minutes for 1½ hours or until the internal temperature registers 160°F (71°C) on an instant-read thermometer.

Place the sour cherries, remaining lemon juice, cherry juice, and brown sugar in a saucepan. Bring the mixture to a slow boil.

In a small bowl, combine the cornstarch and water. Mix well. Slowly stir the cornstarch into the cherry mixture. Turn the heat to low and cook for 3 minutes. Stir in the brandy. Turn off the heat.

When the pork is cooked, remove it from the grill, cover loosely with foil, and let stand 15 minutes before slicing. Reheat the sauce.

Arrange sliced pork on a serving plate and spoon the cherries jubilee sauce over top.

PORK CHOPS WITH APPLE RINGS

2 large apples

Four 9–10 oz (255–300 g)
center-cut pork loin chops
(about ½–¾ inch/1–2 cm thick)

½ cup (125 mL) orange juice

1 Tbsp (15 mL) extra-virgin olive oil

4 tsp (20 mL) chopped fresh basil

1 tsp (5 mL) seasoned salt

½ tsp (2 mL) garlic powder

¼ cup (60 mL) brown sugar

½ tsp (2 mL) ground ginger

¼ tsp (1 mL) lemon pepper

¼ tsp (1 mL) dried basil leaves

CUT EACH APPLE into horizontal slices about a ½-inch (1 cm) thick. Remove the seeds from the center to form rings.

In a bowl, combine the orange juice, olive oil, basil, seasoned salt, and garlic powder.

Place the apple rings flat in a baking dish. Spoon 3 Tbsp (45 mL) of the orange juice mixture over the apple rings. Cover and refrigerate for 2 hours.

Place the pork chops in a resealable plastic bag. Pour the remaining orange juice mixture over the pork chops. Seal tightly, place on a flat plate, and refrigerate for 2 hours.

In a bowl, combine the brown sugar, ginger, lemon pepper, and basil. Mix well.

Remove the apple rings and pork chops from the orange marinade. Pat dry with paper towels. Discard the marinade.

On separate plates, coat the apple rings and pork chops on both sides with the brown sugar mixture.

Preheat the grill on medium (350–450°F/175–230°C) for 10 minutes with the lid closed. Turn one side of the grill off and leave the other side on medium heat to maintain a temperature of 350°F (175°C).

Place the pork chops on the hot side of the grill. Grill about 3 minutes per side to create grid marks. Move the chops to the unlit side of the grate, close the lid, and continue to cook for 20 minutes or until the internal temperature registers 150°F (66°C) on an instant-read thermometer.

Place the apple rings on the hot side of the grill. Grill the apples rings 3 minutes on each side.

Remove the chops from the grill and tent with foil for 10 minutes before serving with the apple rings.

Chefs Create Memories

WE MET ERIC KLEIN, VP Culinary for Wolfgang Puck Catering, on a cruise from Boston to Montreal with the International Food, Wine, and Travel Writers Association (IFWTWA). Eric and his wife, Tori, were part of our group.

One of the cruise stops was Bar Harbor, Maine. Eric disembarked carrying his chef's jacket and his leather kit of chef's knives. Matt McPherson, Executive Chef at The Looking Glass Restaurant in Bar Harbor, was on his day off. The prearranged plan was for the two men to combine talents and create a lunch for our gang of writers as well as the captain of the ship.

After purchasing seafood and vegetables at a local market, Matt toured Eric through the restaurant kitchen, walk-in cooler, and herb garden. Together, they created a menu to highlight fresh Bar Harbor bounty.

We watched in the kitchen as Eric worked beside Matt, offering tips on technique, emphasizing the importance of cooking traditions, and suggesting that once a cook understood the basics of cooking it was possible to do things a little differently—to improvise, and have fun. Matt listened intently, responding to every gem of information with "Yes, Chef."

What impressed us was how, before removing his chef's jacket or packing his knives back into their kit, Eric joined Matt and the rest of the back-of-the-house staff in cleaning up the kitchen. Two chefs, one willing to share what he knew and the other willing to learn, created memories not only for us but for themselves.

MAPLE CITRUS PORK TENDERLOIN

½ cup (125 mL) maple syrup

¾ cup (185 mL) orange juice

2 Tbsp (30 mL) fresh lime juice

1 Tbsp (15 mL) dark rum

1 tsp (5 mL) extra-virgin olive oil

3 lb (1.4 kg) pork tenderloin

IN A BOWL, combine the maple syrup, orange juice, lime juice, dark rum, and olive oil.

Place the tenderloin in a flat glass dish and pour the marinade over top.

Cover the dish. Refrigerate and marinate the pork for 4–6 hours. Turn the pork often to marinate all sides.

Remove the pork from the marinade and save the marinade.

Preheat the grill on medium-high (450–550°F/230–290°C) for 10 minutes with the lid closed. Using a pair of long-handled tongs, oil the grate by wiping it with a piece of folded paper towel dipped lightly in canola oil.

Reduce the heat to medium-low (300–350°F/150–175°C) and place the pork tenderloin on the grate. Close the lid.

Cook for about 20 minutes or until the internal temperature registers 155°F (68°C) on an instant-read thermometer. Turn the tenderloin every 5 minutes.

Transfer the tenderloin to a cutting board, tent loosely with aluminum foil, and rest the meat for 10 minutes before slicing.

In a small saucepan, bring the marinade mixture to a boil over medium-high heat. Boil for 5–10 minutes, stirring constantly.

Slice the pork and drizzle the maple-citrus marinade over top.

Wild Rice is Not Rice

WE DROVE ALONG A narrow, winding road to meet Murray Ratuski at the Shoal Lake Wild Rice Company in Keewatin, Ontario. In the 1930s, Murray's father purchased his first pound of wild rice from the local First Nations people. Today, the rice supply for the family-owned company is harvested in Manitoba, Saskatchewan, and Northern Ontario. Wild rice, also known as Canadian rice, Indian rice, or water oats, is not rice. It is a grass seed.

The building that houses the wild rice processing equipment in Keewatin is ingeniously set on the face of a steep rock cutout. This allows gravity to move the rice through the processing steps. There are a lot of stairs from the upper level, where the green rice arrives by the truckload, to the automatic packaging equipment at the bottom.

Along the gravitational route, the rice is cleaned and parched in huge roasters. This stage gives the wild rice its subtle nutty flavor and aroma. A mechanical husker then separates the kernels from the chaff. Some of the outer bran layer is removed to ensure accurate cooking times. At the bottom level of the operation, the kernels are graded by size and dropped into appropriate bags. The bags are closed, stitched tight, and weighed before being loaded on delivery trucks.

Murray explained the importance of cooking wild rice until the kernels blossom into soft curly swirls. At any stage before that, the rice remains tough and overly chewy.

Wild rice blossoms add not only a naturally gluten-free, cholesterol-free, fat-free, and fiber-filled nutrient to a recipe, but also a gentle texture and nutty flavor.

WILD RICE–STUFFED PORK TENDERLOIN

½ cup (125 mL) wild rice

2 cups (500 mL) cold water

Two 1-lb (450 g) pork tenderloins

½ cup (125 mL) dried cranberries

2 tsp (10 mL) ground ginger

12–16 slices bacon

PLACE THE WILD rice and water in a saucepan. Bring the mixture to a boil. Reduce the heat to medium-low. Cover the saucepan tightly. Continue to boil gently for 30 minutes. Turn off the heat. Keep the saucepan covered for 25–35 minutes or until the grains are soft and curly. Drain the rice, if necessary, and set aside.

Place the tenderloins, narrow-edge up, on a cutting board. Without cutting all the way through, slice the tenderloins down the middle, lengthwise, leaving ½ inch (1 cm) of the meat still intact. Spread the tenderloins open. Pound the meat to get an even thickness.

Add the cranberries to the wild rice. Mix well.

Sprinkle the ginger powder over the surface of the meat.

Place a row of the rice mixture lengthwise along the center of the tenderloins.

Roll the meat over the wild rice. Use toothpicks to hold the wrapped tenderloins together.

For each tenderloin, place 6–8 slices of bacon side by side on a cutting board.

Place the tenderloins in the center of the bacon strips in a perpendicular position.

Wrap the slices of bacon around the tenderloins.

Remove the toothpicks from the tenderloins and use them to secure the ends of the bacon slices.

Preheat the grill on high (550–600°F/290–315°C) for 10 minutes with the lid closed. Using a pair of long-handled tongs, oil the grate by wiping it with a piece of folded paper towel dipped lightly in canola oil. Reduce the heat to medium (350–450°F/175–230°C).

Grill the tenderloins with the lid closed, turning every 5 minutes, for 20–25 minutes, or until the internal temperatures register 145°F (63°C) in the center of the wild rice stuffing on an instant-read thermometer and the bacon is cooked. If the bacon begins to burn, reduce the temperature to medium-low.

Let the tenderloins rest for 10 minutes before slicing into rounds like a jelly roll. Remove the toothpicks before slicing.

In Quartzsite, Home is Where You Park It

THE SONORAN DESERT surrounds the town of Quartzsite, Arizona. The wind-swept pebbled sand is dotted with giant saguaro, prickly pear, cholla, barrel, and fuzzy hedgehog cacti where, over the winter, hundreds of thousands of recreational vehicle owners congregate. Although there are several campgrounds in the vicinity, most visitors choose to pick a cactus in the middle of the desert, park beside it, and call it home.

In January and February, the entire 36 square miles (58 square kilometers) of town transform into an enormous flea market. Among the tents and trailers, lean-tos and buildings, everything from tires and solar panels to clothing and kitchenware is for sale. At the same time, an annual gem show is a mecca for visitors and exhibitors interested in rocks, gems, mineral specimens, and fossils.

If a particular item cannot be found in Quartzsite, it is unlikely to be available anywhere.

Beyond the bustle of town, there are roads and trails ideal for off-roading, rock climbing, and hiking in the desert and surrounding mountains. Early every morning dirt bikes, ATVs, SUVs, and Jeeps head out for a day of bouncing over rocks.

Glistening with suntan lotion, carrying water bottles, and avoiding critters that live in holes at the bases of scrubby bushes, we hiked along a dry riverbed and stumbled upon petroglyphs that, in Arizona, are believed to be thousands of years old. They are found on rock faces in areas where early humans paused long enough to record events, leave directions, or maybe even write recipes.

THICK GINGER-BEER PORK CHOPS

1 cup (250 mL) beer (any style will do)	¼ cup (60 mL) orange juice	½ tsp (2 mL) garlic powder
1 Tbsp (15 mL) brown sugar	1 Tbsp (15 mL) ginger marmalade	Two 9–10 oz (255–300 g) pork chops (about 1¼ inches/3 cm thick)
1 Tbsp (15 mL) Dijon mustard	2 bay leaves	

IN A BOWL, combine the beer, brown sugar, mustard, orange juice, marmalade, bay leaves, and garlic powder. Mix well. Pour the mixture into a large resealable plastic bag.

Add the pork chops to the bag. Seal the bag tightly and place the bag flat on a plate in the refrigerator. Marinate chops for 12–24 hours. Turn the bag over at least once while the pork marinates.

Preheat the grill on high (550–600°F/290–315°C) for 10 minutes with the lid closed. Using a pair of long-handled tongs, oil the grate by wiping it with a piece of folded paper towel dipped lightly in canola oil.

Remove the chops from the marinade. Discard the marinade.

Turn one side of the grill off to prepare the grill for indirect cooking.

Place the pork chops on the grate over the direct-heat side of the grill to create grill marks. Sear the chops for about 3 minutes per side with the lid closed.

Transfer the chops to the indirect-heat side of the grill and cook, with the lid closed, for about 10–15 minutes per side or until the internal temperature registers 150°F (66°C) on an instant-read thermometer inserted horizontally into the center of the chops, away from the bone.

Transfer the chops to a platter, tent with foil, and let rest for 10 minutes before serving.

Calgary's Patina Maze

IN CALGARY, ALBERTA, the streets run north and south, avenues east and west. It sounds simple. On our first venture into downtown, we sat at a traffic light at the corner of 4th Avenue SW and 4th Street SW. We were surrounded by buildings, did not have a GPS, and could not see the mountains for direction. North, south, east, and west were a mystery to us. We were scheduled for an early morning television interview on 7th Avenue SW. When we turned onto 7th Avenue, we found ourselves driving on the track of the C-train, the city's light-rail transit system.

Unwilling to park the motor home in harm's way, we pulled along the side of the building, extended the motor home's slide-out room, and set up the ingredients for the breakfast recipe that we were going to prepare on camera.

A law enforcement officer arrived to write us a ticket with the words "Tow it" scrawled across the top. To avoid being towed, we backed our behemoth into a laneway behind the studio. Again, we extended the slide-out room and set the breakfast ingredients and dishes on the kitchen counter. Moments before we were to go on air, a man pulled up beside the motor home and shouted, "Move it." We ignored him.

Later the same day, we had a television interview at a studio on Patina Rise. We circled Patina Drive, Patina Close, and Patina Avenue several times. Finally, like a maze, one of the streets pointed the way to a spectacular view of Calgary. And with that, we were on Patina Rise.

SLOW & SUCCULENT BOSTON BUTT ROAST

3 Tbsp (45 mL) brown sugar

1 tsp (5 mL) garlic powder

1 tsp (5 mL) dried rosemary leaves, crumbled

½ tsp (2 mL) salt

½ tsp (2 mL) pepper

4 lb (1.8 kg) boneless pork shoulder roast (Boston butt)

At least 2 cups (500 mL) apple juice

At least 2 cups (500 mL) water

½–¾ cup (125–185 mL) barbecue sauce, to finish

IN A SMALL bowl, combine the brown sugar, garlic powder, rosemary, salt, and pepper. Rub the mixture over the surface of the roast.

Set up the grill to cook the roast with indirect heat by placing a deep drip pan under the grate on one side of the grill. Combine the apple juice and water in a measuring cup. Pour the apple juice and water mixture into the drip pan.

Preheat the grill on medium (350–450°F/175–230°C) for 10 minutes with the lid closed. Using a pair of long-handled tongs, oil the grate by wiping it with a piece of folded paper towel dipped lightly in canola oil.

Pour extra apple juice and water into the drip pan if necessary to prevent the pan from cooking dry. Place the roast, fat-side down, on the grate above the drip pan. Turn the heat off under the drip pan. Close the lid.

Cook the pork roast for 4–4½ hours or until the internal temperature registers 170°F (77°C) on an instant-read thermometer. Turn the roast over every hour.

Transfer the pork to a cutting board. Tent with aluminum foil for 20 minutes before slicing. Slather slices with barbecue sauce.

Our Mug Up in Lunenburg

AS PART OF a walking tour of Lunenburg, Nova Scotia, we sampled some of the makings of a "mug up": Lunenburg pudding, Solomon Gundy, smoked mackerel, smoked herring, smoked salmon, hard tack, caplin, dulse, and spicy molasses cookies. A good mug up was a seaman's reward, a hearty snack at the end of a hard day.

David Fancy was known for making the best Solomon Gundy, a local version of marinated herring. When we met David near Kraustown, Nova Scotia, he explained that he cut all his herring by hand. Signs on his small blue delivery truck promoted the high levels of omega-3 fatty acids in his products. We followed David down several backroads to our next food stop, Greek's Quality Meats, the makers of the famous Lunenburg pudding.

We chatted with Richard Greek, whose father started the Bridgewater, Nova Scotia, meat business. The company has a reputation for genuine Lunenburg pudding, a cooked sausage traditionally served as part of a meal with sauerkraut and boiled potatoes. Although produced year-round, Lunenburg pudding is most popular at Christmastime.

On our way back to the Lunenburg Board of Trade Campground, we stopped to chat with Kevin Rhodenizer, the owner of Krispi Kraut Nova Scotia sauerkraut. All natural, his mild-flavored sauerkraut includes only three ingredients: cabbage, salt, and water.

It may not be Lunenburg pudding with all the fixings of a real mug up, but our Sausages on a Bed of Kraut recipe (see next page) just begs for boiled potatoes on the side.

SAUSAGES ON A BED OF KRAUT

2 cups (500 mL) sweet apple cider
or apple juice

1 large onion

2 cups (500 mL) sauerkraut

1–1¼ lb (450–600 g) fresh pork
sausages

Canola oil (for brushing)

POUR THE APPLE cider into a deep frying pan. Cut the onion into thick slices. Add the onion slices to the cider. Place the sauerkraut on top of the onions.

Bring the contents of the frying pan to a boil over medium-high heat.

Prick each sausage 2–3 times with just the very tip of a sharp knife. Add the sausages to the cider, onions, and sauerkraut.

Partially cover the frying pan with a lid. Turn the heat down to medium and cook the sausages for 30 minutes.

Preheat the grill on high (550–600°F/290–315°C) for 10 minutes with the lid closed. Using a pair of long-handled tongs, oil the grate by wiping it with a piece of folded paper towel dipped lightly in canola oil.

Brush the sausages with canola oil.

Place the sausages on the grate and grill for 4–6 minutes with the lid open. Turn the sausages often in order to grill them evenly.

Place the hot onions and sauerkraut on a serving dish. Arrange the grilled sausages on top of the sauerkraut.

Island with Attitude

CHARLOTTETOWN, PRINCE EDWARD ISLAND, was the site of a conference in 1864 to discuss a union of Canada's Maritime provinces. John A. MacDonald and George-Étienne Cartier, who would work together to eventually make the case for Confederation, saw an opportunity to further their cause to create a nation. No one greeted them at the Charlottetown dock but, in spite of the snubbing, the conclusion to the conference was an agreement to unite the British North America colonies into a federal union.

Prince Edward Island did not join the union until 1873. One of the comments of the day was, "So, I see the mainland has decided to join us."

Today, the Confederation Bridge, an S-shaped, 8-mile (13 kilometer) stretch of raised highway, joins the mainland of Canada to the island. The drive across the Northumberland Strait from Cape Jourimain, New Brunswick, to Borden-Carleton, PEI, took us just over 10 minutes. An alternative is an 80-minute ferry ride. The bridge, like the ferry, only charges a toll one-way, upon exiting the island.

Prince Edward Island is the largest potato-producing province in Canada. The potato industry on the island produces seed potatoes, baking potatoes, fresh table potatoes, and processed potatoes in the form of French fries, potato chips, dehydrated potatoes, canned potatoes, and potato flour.

Sometimes we appreciate the island's potatoes in the form of fresh-cut fries and poutine, and sometimes we make an entire meal by stuffing a jumbo baked potato with meat, vegetables, and cheese (see next page).

JUMBO STUFFED BAKED POTATO

4 large baking potatoes

Canola oil (for brushing)

1½ lb (700 g) boneless pork loin roast

1½ cups (375 mL) barbecue sauce

1 tsp (5 mL) hot sauce

¼ cup (60 mL) Worcestershire sauce

¼ cup (60 mL) soy sauce

¼ cup (60 mL) butter or margarine

½ cup (125 mL) sour cream

2 cups (500 mL) finely shredded cheddar cheese

2 green onions, chopped

WASH THE POTATOES and prick them with a fork.

Preheat the grill on medium-high (450–550°F/230–290°C) for 10 minutes with the lid closed. Using a pair of long-handled tongs, oil the grate by wiping it with a piece of folded paper towel dipped lightly in canola oil.

Lightly brush canola oil over the pork loin.

Sear the pork loin for 2 minutes on both sides with the lid closed.

Turn the heat down to medium-low (300–350°F/150–175°C) and place the potatoes on the grate beside the pork loin.

Turn the roast and potatoes every 10–15 minutes throughout the cooking time.

Cook for about 40 minutes with the lid closed, or until the internal temperature of the meat registers 160°F (71°C) on an instant-read thermometer and the potatoes are cooked through.

Remove meat from the grill. Continue to cook the potatoes, if necessary.

Transfer meat to a cutting board. Tent meat loosely with aluminum foil and let it rest for 15 minutes.

In a saucepan, combine the barbecue sauce, hot sauce, Worcestershire sauce, and soy sauce. Set aside.

Cut the meat into bite-sized squares and add to the barbecue sauce mixture. Stir over medium heat for about 2–3 minutes or until the sauce is hot and bubbling.

Cut each baked potato open. Place butter, sour cream, and cheese inside each potato. Spoon the hot pork mixture over top and sprinkle with the chopped green onions.

COLUMBIA, MISSOURI, is midway between Kansas City and St. Louis on Interstate 70. Travelers who pull off the highway discover that the city is not what they expect. More a neighborhood than a city, Columbia enjoys all the positives and high energy of a university town.

The red brick buildings and shady trees of three campuses—the University of Missouri, Columbia College, and Stephens College—are intimately located on three sides of the square mile that embraces downtown. Stephens College is the second-oldest women's college in the country. Columbia College began as the first women's college west of the Mississippi and became co-ed in 1970. The University of Missouri, affectionately celebrated as Mizzou, was founded in 1839. Known for its School of Journalism, students staff the city's morning newspaper as reporters, designers, and editors. Mort Walker's comic strip character, Beetle Bailey, patterned after the artist's Mizzou fraternity friends, can be found sitting, statuesque, at a picnic table on campus.

Public benches and flower installations merge to form street art. Graffiti beautifies utility boxes. Neon art decorates parking garages. Two sets of Greek columns connect the Court House and City Hall with the campus of the University of Missouri. There are over 50 miles (80 kilometers) of trails within the city that link to the Katy Trail State Park, the longest rails-to-trails project in the United States. A food truck purveys pulled pork, kale slaw, and fried pimento cheese balls. On request, an ice cream parlor transforms a cup of ice cream into a frozen cocktail. Trendy menus draw crowds to bistros, grills, brewpubs, and casual dining rooms. Columbia's Convention and Visitors Bureau promotes the city as "what you unexpect." And it's true.

Pork steaks are a local favorite and a staple of St. Louis-style barbecue.

SMOKED PORK STEAKS

6 Tbsp (90 mL) prepared mustard

6 Tbsp (90 mL) brown sugar

½ tsp (2 mL) coarsely ground pepper

Four 12-oz (340 g) pork shoulder blade steaks

At least ¼ cup (60 mL) barbecue sauce

IN A BOWL, combine the mustard, brown sugar, and pepper.

Place the pork steaks on a plate and spread the mustard sauce on both sides of the pork. Refrigerate for 1–2 hours.

Using hickory wood, preheat the smoker to low (180°F/82°C). Smoke the pork steaks for 1½ hours.

Remove the steaks and lightly brush both sides with barbecue sauce. Wrap the steaks individually in aluminum foil.

Bring the temperature in the smoker up to medium (225°F/105°C) and put the foil-wrapped steaks on the grate. Cook the steaks for 1 hour or until the internal temperature registers 160°F (71°C) on an instant-read thermometer. Turn the foil packets over half way through the cooking time.

For a firmer texture, remove the pork steaks from the foil during the last 15 minutes and put them directly on the grate. Discard any liquid in the foil.

SMOKED APPLE CIDER–MARINATED RIBS

Two 2½-lb (1.1 kg) racks pork side ribs

2 tsp (10 mL) dry mustard

1 Tbsp (15 mL) finely chopped fresh ginger

1 tsp (5 mL) apple cider vinegar

1 cup (250 mL) sweet apple cider

2 garlic cloves, finely chopped

1 Tbsp (15 mL) canola oil

CUT THE RIBS in half to fit in a container for marinating.

In a bowl, combine the dry mustard, ginger, and vinegar. Stir to a smooth paste. Add the cider, garlic, and oil. Mix well.

Pour half the marinade into a large flat baking dish. Place the ribs in the marinade. Pour the remaining marinade over the ribs. Cover the dish. Marinate in the refrigerator for 12–24 hours. Turn the ribs over 2–3 times while they marinate.

Remove the ribs from the marinade. Discard the marinade.

Cook the ribs in a smoker at medium (275°F/140°C) for about 3½ hours or until the meat registers 180°F (82°C) on an instant-read thermometer. Turn the ribs over halfway through the cooking time. A simple way to test doneness is to grasp 2 bones and pull them in opposite directions. If the meat is tender enough to pull the ribs apart and the ends of the bones are protruding, the ribs are done.

Life and Death in Savannah

WHEN VISITING SAVANNAH, Georgia, our tour guide enthralled us with deadly details about the city, we took him at his word because he worked for the historical society. He said Savannah was haunted by tragic happenings from the city's history. Yellow plague. Fire. Flood. Tornadoes. British invasions. The American Revolution.

"When contractors in the city break ground for development purposes, they inevitably find human remains," he said. "In the past, nobody respected the dead."

Chief Tomochichi was the 17th-century chief of the Yamacraws, a tribe formed from a group of people from the Yamasee and Creek aboriginal communities. Tomochichi was a key connection between Savannah's aboriginal population and its English settlers. Chief Tomochichi gave land to General James Oglethorpe, who established Savannah. Tomochichi is buried in Wright Square but the monument in the center of the square is dedicated to someone else. In Monterey Square, Casimir Pulaski, who was mortally wounded during the Siege of Savannah, is honored. However, the story is that Pulaski died at sea, so no one knows who is buried where he is supposed to be. No wonder some Savannah houses have a special blue paint, haint, on doors and windowsills that is meant to confuse evil spirits and keep them at bay. Haints are spirits trapped between the world of the living and the world of the dead.

The origin of Brunswick Stew (see next page) is also a mystery. Georgia, Virginia, and North Carolina all claim to be its birthplace. Some say a stew is not Brunswick stew unless squirrel is an ingredient. But one thing everyone agrees on is that the stew is not ready until the stirring paddle stands on its own, straight up in the pot.

SMOKED PORK BRUNSWICK STEW

¼ cup (60 mL) brown sugar

1 tsp (5 mL) garlic powder

3 lb (1.4 kg) boneless pork shoulder roast

2 large potatoes, peeled

¼ cup (60 mL) butter

2 medium onions, peeled and diced

3 cups (750 mL) chicken broth

One 28-oz (796 mL) can diced tomatoes with liquid

One 19-oz (540 mL) can butter beans or lima beans, drained

One 14-oz (398 mL) can cream-style corn

1 Tbsp (15 mL) white sugar

1½ Tbsp (23 mL) apple cider vinegar

1 tsp (5 mL) salt

¼ tsp (1 mL) pepper

¼ tsp (1 mL) cayenne pepper

2 Tbsp (30 mL) Worcestershire sauce

IN A SMALL bowl, combine the brown sugar and garlic powder. Generously rub the mixture over the pork.

Preheat the smoker to medium-high (300°F/150°C) with hickory wood.

Cook the pork, fat-side up, for about 4 hours or until the internal temperature registers 170°F (77°C) on an instant-read thermometer.

Transfer the pork to a cutting board. Chop the meat into pieces no bigger than 2 × 4 inches (5 × 10 cm). Set aside in the refrigerator.

Boil the potatoes until tender. Drain and mash the potatoes with a fork.

Melt the butter in a large soup pot over medium heat. Add the onions. Cook for 10 minutes or until the onions are tender. Stir occasionally.

Add the chicken broth to the onions. Stir in the pork.

Increase heat to medium-high. Cook and stir the pork for 5 minutes.

Add all remaining ingredients but the Worcestershire sauce. Stir until the mixture reaches a boil.

Reduce heat to medium to hold at a slow boil. Stir in the Worcestershire sauce.

At this point, the Brunswick stew must be stirred every 3–5 minutes to prevent sticking.

Continue to cook slowly for 2–3 hours or until no liquid is evident.

As the stew thickens, reduce heat to medium-low and increase the stirring to every 2 minutes.

During the last half-hour of cooking, reduce heat to low and stir constantly.

The stew is ready when the consistency has become very thick, the meat has broken down into thin strands, and the spoon stands up on its own in the pot.

SMOKED BOLOGNA

2–2½ lb (0.9–1.1 kg) chunk of bologna

2 Tbsp (30 mL) prepared mustard

¼ cup (60 mL) brown sugar

1 tsp (5 mL) onion powder

½ tsp (2 mL) dry mustard

1 cup (250 mL) apple juice

REMOVE THE CASING from the bologna. Cut cross-slits into the bologna about ½ inch (1 cm) deep to form a diamond pattern all the way around. Do not score the ends.

Place the bologna in a baking dish.

Spread a layer of the prepared mustard over the entire surface of the bologna.

In a bowl, combine the brown sugar, onion powder, and dry mustard. Pat the brown sugar mixture over the prepared mustard on the bologna.

Pour the apple juice around the base of the bologna in the baking dish.

Preheat the smoker to medium (225°F/105°C). Place the baking dish on the grate. Smoke for 3–3½ hours. Spoon the liquid in the dish over the bologna every hour.

Transfer to a cutting board. Cool for 15 minutes before slicing thinly for sandwiches or thickly as an entrée. Can also be refrigerated and served cold. To create grid marks or to reheat, thickly sliced bologna can be placed on a hot grill for about 1–2 minutes per side.

BEEF

PAPRIKA PRIME RIB ROAST

¼ cup (60 mL) paprika

2 Tbsp (30 mL) garlic powder

2 tsp (10 mL) onion powder

2 tsp (10 mL) cumin

2 tsp (10 mL) dry mustard

2 tsp (10 mL) pepper

1 tsp (5 mL) salt

8-lb (3.5 kg) 3-rib prime rib roast

IN A BOWL, mix the paprika, garlic powder, onion powder, cumin, dry mustard, pepper, and salt.

Pat the roast dry with paper towels.

Massage the paprika mixture onto the beef, evenly coating the entire surface.

Let the roast stand at room temperature for 30 minutes before grilling.

Preheat the grill on high (550–600°F/290–315°C) for 10 minutes with the lid closed. Using a pair of long-handled tongs, oil the grate by wiping it with a piece of folded paper towel dipped lightly in canola oil.

Prepare the grill for indirect cooking. Turn one side of the grill off and reduce the heat on the other side to medium-low (300–350°F/150–175°C) to maintain a temperature of about 325°F (160°C).

Place the rib roast, fat-side up, on the unlit side of the grate.

Cook for about 14–16 minutes per pound, or until the internal temperature registers 135°F (57°C) for medium-rare on an instant-read thermometer, or to desired doneness.

Transfer the roast to a cutting board and tent with aluminum foil for 15 minutes to allow the juices to accumulate and the flavors to blend. The roast will continue cooking for a short time after it is removed from the grill.

To carve a prime rib roast, turn it bone side up and cut the bones away from the meat.

Turn the roast over and carve into serving slices.

BRAISING BEEF RIBS

4 lb (1.8 kg) meaty braising beef rib bones

2 Tbsp (30 mL) brown sugar

1 Tbsp (15 mL) smoked paprika

½ tsp (2 mL) salt

1 tsp (5 mL) pepper

Molasses Sauce (see page 230)

TRIM EXCESS FAT from the beef ribs.

In a bowl, combine the brown sugar, paprika, salt, and pepper.

Place the ribs in a large flat dish. Rub the brown sugar mixture over the ribs. Cover the ribs with plastic wrap and refrigerate for 2–3 hours.

Preheat the grill on high (550–600°F/290–315°C) for 10 minutes with the lid closed. Using a pair of long-handled tongs, oil the grate by wiping it with a piece of folded paper towel dipped lightly in canola oil.

Reduce the heat to medium (350–450°F/175–230°C) on one side of the grill. Turn the heat off on the other side.

Place the ribs side by side on a large piece of heavy-duty aluminum foil brushed with canola oil.

Tightly wrap the foil over the ribs keeping the ribs side by side. Cover tightly with a second piece of foil to prevent leaking. Place the packages on the unlit portion of the grill. Close the lid.

Cook the ribs for 2½ hours at 350–375°F (175–190°C). Using oven mitts or a large lifter, rotate and turn the ribs every 45 minutes.

Transfer the ribs to a large platter. Do not turn off the grill. Set the temperature on both sides of the grill to medium (350–450°F/175–230°C).

Remove the foil from the ribs. Discard the foil. Slather the ribs on both sides generously with the Molasses Sauce.

Oil the grate and place the ribs directly on the grate. Grill for about 10 minutes, turning every few minutes so they don't burn. The ribs should be crunchy and browned on the outside but still tender and moist inside.

Memories of Temecula Wine Country

SEVERAL OF OUR fellow food, wine, and travel writer friends live in Temecula, California, a city an hour north of San Diego. There, to the benefit of grape growers, the sun shines intensely almost every day. Rows of grapevines follow the curves of rolling hillsides. Most Temecula vineyards are small and family owned, which makes the wine experience personal for everyone.

The RV Park at the Pechanga Resort and Casino, the largest resort-casino combination in the state of California, was our home for a brief while. The facility blends into the landscape with indigenous flowers, plants, and native cultural artifacts. Pechanga's chefs offer five-star food.

In the heart of Temecula, we wandered through Old Town, a vibrant frontier town with 21st-century tastes. A spice store, olive oil shop, theater, boutiques, and eclectic trendy restaurants fuse with collectible stores and historic buildings. Trucks parked on the street offer fresh vegetables and fruit. We sniffed spices and tasted olive oils, met shop owners, and posed for photos. Our footsteps resonated on the sun-bleached boardwalk.

The Temecula wineries are places where friends meet at the end of each day. With so many choices of vineyard, the happy hour venue rotates regularly. Each time we met to swirl and sip, the group expanded. Sitting in lounge chairs overlooking grapevines and watching the sunset, we shared stories about wine, travel, and food. Even though our time in Temecula was short, the sense of camaraderie was powerful.

We love cooking with wine. Our melt-in-your-mouth Reverse-Seared New York Strip (see next page) is our idea of the perfect steak.

REVERSE-SEARED NEW YORK STRIP

One ¼-lb (125 g) butter stick

Two 1¾-2 inch (4.5-5 cm) thick strip loin steaks

Sea salt, to taste

Coarsely ground pepper, to taste

2 shallots, chopped

2 tsp (10 mL) chopped fresh tarragon

1 cup (250 mL) red wine

CUT THE BUTTER into 16 squares about ¼-inch (6 mm) thick. Place the squares side by side on a plate and freeze.

Place the steaks on a large plate. Lightly sprinkle salt and pepper over both sides. Cover with plastic wrap. Refrigerate for 30 minutes to allow the steaks to absorb the seasonings before grilling. Remove the steaks from the refrigerator 15–30 minutes before grilling.

Preheat the grill on medium (350–450°F/175–230°C) for 10 minutes with the lid closed.

Prepare the grill for indirect cooking. Turn one side of the grill off. Reduce the other side to medium-low (300–350°F/150–175°C) heat to maintain a temperature of 250–300°F (120–150°C).

Using a pair of long-handled tongs, oil the unlit side of the grate by wiping it with a piece of paper towel dipped lightly in canola oil.

Place the steaks on the unlit side of the grate. Place 2 frozen butter squares on the top of each steak.

Maintaining a grill temperature of 250–300°F (120–150°C), cook the steaks, with the lid closed, for 40–45 minutes, or to 10 degrees less than the final desired doneness. For example, for a final temperature of 135°F (57°C) for medium-rare, remove the steaks from the grill when the internal temperature registers 125°F (52°C) on an instant-read thermometer or on a meat probe inserted into the side of a steak.

Transfer the steaks to a platter and tent loosely with aluminum foil.

Place a cast iron frying pan on the grill grate. Turn all the burners to high (550–600°F/290–315°C) and heat the grill to a searing 600°F (315°C) with the lid closed.

Place 6 frozen butter squares in the hot frying pan. When the butter sizzles add the steaks.

With the lid open, sear the steaks about 2 minutes on each side, or until the internal temperature registers 135°F (57°C) for medium-rare, or 140°F (60°C) for medium, on an instant-read thermometer.

Transfer the steaks to a platter and tent loosely with aluminum foil. Let rest for at least 10 minutes, or until the sauce is prepared.

Reduce the grill heat to medium (350–450°F/175–230°C).

Add 6 frozen butter squares and the shallots to the pan. Stir and cook the shallots for about a minute or until tender. Add the tarragon and wine. Stir and cook until the sauce reduces to half.

Trickle the sauce over the steaks before serving.

MARINATED SIRLOIN STEAK

Two 1-lb (450 g) top sirloin steaks

½ cup (125 mL) peeled and chopped onion

3 garlic cloves, chopped

½ cup (125 mL) extra-virgin olive oil

¼ cup (60 mL) red wine vinegar

2 Tbsp (30 mL) soy sauce

1 Tbsp (15 mL) Worcestershire sauce

1 tsp (5 mL) Dijon mustard

½ tsp (2 mL) hot sauce

¼ tsp (1 mL) sea salt

¼ tsp (1 mL) coarsely ground pepper

PLACE THE STEAKS flat in a shallow, glass dish.

In a bowl, combine the remaining ingredients. Mix well.

Pour the mixture over the steak. Turn the meat to coat both sides. Cover and refrigerate 12–24 hours. Turn the steaks once or twice while marinating.

Preheat the grill on high (550–600°F/290–315°C) for 10 minutes with the lid closed. Using a pair of long-handled tongs, oil the grate by wiping it with a piece of folded paper towel dipped lightly in canola oil.

Remove steaks from the marinade. Discard marinade.

With the lid closed, grill the steaks for about 5 minutes on each side or until the internal temperature registers 135°F (57°C) for medium-rare on an instant-read thermometer.

Transfer the steaks to a cutting board. Let rest for 10 minutes before serving.

Scenic Route like No Other

WATERFALLS, LAKES, ANCIENT twisted trees climbing over rocks, a glacier clinging to a distant mountain slope, and purple fireweed: all this on a breathtaking 62-mile (100 kilometer) stretch of South Klondike Highway 2 between Whitehorse, Yukon Territory, and Skagway, Alaska, the gateway to the Klondike Gold Rush of 1898.

Every turn in the road produced more of the unexpected. Our first stop was Emerald Lake, where light waves reflect off the white lake bottom to give the surface of the water a rainbow sheen. At Carcross, we hiked the high dunes of the world's smallest desert. Once the location of a glacial lake, monstrous mounds of sandy-bottom material were left behind when the ice melted. The desert may be small, but from the highest point we could see Lake Bennett, the distant waterway that played an important part in the Gold Rush. This was where prospectors arrived by boat from California and coastal British Columbia to begin their excruciating overland hike to gold country, bearing food supplies and heavy equipment like stoves on their backs.

Skagway still looks like a gold rush town with its boardwalks and old wood-framed buildings. The population has dwindled from the tens of thousands of gold-frenzied fortune-seeking prospectors to its present year-round population of less than 1,000.

The big difference now is that people arrive by cruise ship, if they aren't fortunate enough to drive South Klondike Highway 2.

DIAMOND-GRILLED STRIP LOIN STEAK

½ cup (125 mL) apple cider vinegar

2 Tbsp (30 mL) extra-virgin olive oil

1 Tbsp (15 mL) soy sauce

1 Tbsp (15 mL) Worcestershire sauce

½ tsp (2 mL) hot sauce

2 Tbsp (30 mL) Dijon mustard

3 cloves garlic, finely chopped

½ cup (125 mL) brown sugar

Four 1-inch (2.5 cm) thick strip loin steaks

IN A BOWL, combine all ingredients but the steaks. Whisk.

Place the steaks in a large resealable plastic bag.

Pour the marinade over the steaks. Tightly seal the bag. Turn and shake the bag to coat the meat with the marinade.

Place the bag flat on a plate in the refrigerator. Marinate for 24 hours. Turn the bag once or twice while marinating. Discard the marinade after using.

Preheat the grill on high (550–600°F/290–315°C) for 10 minutes with the lid closed. Using a pair of long-handled tongs, oil the grate by wiping it with a piece of folded paper towel dipped lightly in canola oil.

Place the steaks on the grill, immediately after oiling the grate. To create diamond-shaped grill marks place the steaks at a 45 degree angle on the cooking grate. Cook for 3–4 minutes. Rotate the steaks to a 45 degree angle the opposite way without turning them over. Grill for 2–3 minutes. Turn the steaks over and repeat the procedure to create diamond-shaped grill marks on the second side. Cook to desired doneness.

The steaks will be medium-rare when the internal temperature registers 135°F (57°C) on an instant-read thermometer.

Transfer the steaks to a platter and tent loosely with aluminum foil. Allow steaks to rest for 5–10 minutes before serving.

MARINATED BEEF KABOBS

½ cup (125 mL) canola oil

½ cup (125 mL) apple cider vinegar

1½ Tbsp (23 mL) Worcestershire sauce

½ tsp (2 mL) salt

½ tsp (2 mL) coarsely ground pepper

1 clove garlic, minced

½ Tbsp (7.5 mL) dried basil leaves

¼ tsp (1 mL) crushed red pepper

1½ lb (750 g) thick cut sirloin steak

COMBINE ALL INGREDIENTS but the steak. Mix well.

Cut the steak into 1-inch (2.5 cm) cubes.

Pour the marinade into a large, resealable plastic bag. Add the cubed beef. Seal the bag tightly. Toss and shake the beef to coat every piece with the marinade. Place the bag flat on a plate in the refrigerator. Marinate for 12–24 hours. Turn the bag over at least once while the beef marinates.

Remove the beef from the marinade. Discard the marinade.

Thread the beef cubes onto metal skewers, or on wooden skewers that have soaked in water for 30 minutes. Do not squeeze the cubes too tightly together.

Preheat the grill on high (550–600°F/290–315°C) for 10 minutes with the lid closed. Using a pair of long-handled tongs, oil the grate by wiping it with a piece of folded paper towel dipped lightly in canola oil.

Grill the beef for 10–12 minutes with the lid closed. Turn the kabobs every few minutes to brown the meat on all sides.

PHONY FILLETS

8 oz (230 g) packaged stuffing mix

1 egg

1 lb (450 g) ground beef

1 Tbsp (15 mL) Worcestershire sauce

¼ cup (60 mL) sliced black olives, finely chopped

7–8 slices bacon

¼ cup (60 mL) blue cheese, crumbled

PREPARE THE STUFFING according to package instructions. Set aside.

In a large bowl, beat the egg. Add the stuffing, beef, Worcestershire sauce, and olives. Mix well. Divide the mixture into 5 equal portions. Form 1-inch (2.5 cm) thick patties. Make a wide, shallow indent in the center of each patty to prevent puffing up while cooking.

Trim the bacon slices to match the height of the patties.

Wrap each fillet with 1½ strips of bacon and secure the bacon with a toothpick.

Preheat the grill on high (550–600°F/290–315°C) for 10 minutes with the lid closed. Using a pair of long-handled tongs, oil the grate by wiping it with a piece of folded paper towel dipped lightly in canola oil.

Brush the top and bottom of the fillets with canola oil and grill, with the lid closed, for 6–7 minutes on each side or until an instant-read thermometer registers 160°F (71°C).

Top the meat with crumbled blue cheese during the last few minutes of cooking.

STEAK & THREE-PEPPER STIR FRY

3 garlic cloves, finely chopped

2 tsp (10 mL) dried basil leaves

½ cup (125 mL) extra-virgin olive oil

¼ cup (60 mL) red wine vinegar

1 lb (450 g) thick sirloin steak,
cut into cubes

1 small red bell pepper, cut into chunks

1 small green bell pepper,
cut into chunks

1 small yellow bell pepper,
cut into chunks

1 small mild onion, cut into chunks

1 cup (250 mL) pineapple tidbits,
drained

6 medium-sized mushrooms,
cut in half

1 Tbsp (15 mL) extra-virgin olive oil

¼ tsp (1 mL) salt

¼ tsp (1 mL) pepper

IN A BOWL, combine the garlic, basil, olive oil, and red wine vinegar.

Place the steak cubes in a large, resealable plastic bag. Pour the marinade over the meat. Seal the bag. Shake the bag to coat the meat. Place the bag flat on a plate and refrigerate for 24 hours.

In a large bowl, combine the peppers, onion, pineapple, mushrooms, olive oil, salt, and pepper. Toss to coat the vegetables with the olive oil.

Remove the steak from the refrigerator and discard the marinade.

Place an oiled wok on the grill grate. Preheat the grill on high (550–600°F/290–315°C) for 10 minutes with the lid closed. Reduce the grill temperature to medium-high (450–550°F/230–290°C).

Add the cubed steak to the wok. Brown the meat for 2 minutes on each side with the lid closed.

Add the vegetables. Stir gently to mix the meat with the vegetables.

Close the lid and cook for 10–15 minutes or until the vegetables are tender-crisp. Stir every 4–5 minutes.

The Horseshoe Falls

THE NIAGARA RIVER drains water from the upper Great Lakes to Lake Ontario. Along the route, there just happens to be a spectacular waterfall in the shape of a horseshoe. Millions of people visit Niagara Falls, Ontario, annually. The river beneath the falls is as deep as the falls are high.

Beyond the natural beauty of the falls, or perhaps because of it, the city of Niagara Falls has always attracted a mixed barrel of visitors. Actually, it's difficult to think of Niagara falls without thinking of barrels, since they were the traditional vessel used to conquer the falls.

In 1901, Mrs. Annie Taylor, a 63-year old school-teacher, became the first person to go over the falls in a whiskey barrel. The barrel appeared close to the Canadian shore 15 minutes after it dropped to the base of the falls. To everyone's surprise, Annie emerged from the barrel intact, save for a cut on her forehead that she received while exiting the barrel. French tightrope walker Charles Blondin, also known as the Great Blondin, crossed the Niagara Gorge on a tightrope several times, once with a man on his back. An Italian woman walked across backwards. There were others too, but since 1912 daredevil stunts over the falls have only been allowed once in a generation, as a way to pay tribute to the stunting history that assisted in making Niagara Falls a top global tourism destination.

STRIP LOIN ROULADEN

1 Tbsp (15 mL) canola oil + extra
(for brushing)

1 medium, mild onion, thinly sliced
into rings

Four 6–8 oz (170–230 g) strip loin
steaks (¼ inch/6 mm thick)

4 tsp (20 mL) prepared mustard

½ tsp (2 mL) salt

½ tsp (2 mL) pepper

½ tsp (2 mL) garlic powder

8 thin slices dill pickle

4 strips bacon, cut in half, cooked

HEAT OIL IN a frying pan over medium heat. Add the onion rings and cook until tender. Set aside to cool.

Place the strip loins on a cutting board. Trim excess fat and sinew from the edges.

Pound the steaks with a meat mallet as thinly as possible, without tearing the meat, to a minimum of 5 inches (12 cm) in width.

Brush mustard on the top side of the meat. Sprinkle with salt, pepper, and garlic powder.

Place one-quarter of the onions on the widest end of each of the strip loins. Top the onions with 2 slices of pickle. Top the pickle with 2 pieces of bacon.

Roll the meat up and over the fillings. Continue to roll while pulling the sides of the meat up over the fillings as much as possible. Secure the seams with toothpicks.

Preheat the grill on medium (350–450°F/175–230°C) for 10 minutes with the lid closed. Turn one side of the grill off and leave the other side on medium to maintain a temperature of about 350°F (175°C).

Brush canola oil over the *rouladen* and place the rolls on the hot side of the grill to sear for about 2 minutes on each side or until grid marks appear.

Transfer the seared rolls to the unlit side of the grill. Cook for 1 hour.

Transfer the *rouladen* to a platter and remove the toothpicks.

We Said No to Bob at Lutes Casino

IT IS DIFFICULT to say what we noticed first, whether it was the parachutist falling through the ceiling or the electrical lineman strapped up a pole. There is not an inch of space on any wall in Lutes Casino in the heart of downtown Yuma that isn't covered with memorabilia. Nor a tile in the ceiling that doesn't have something swinging from it. Signed photos of Marilyn Monroe, Babe Ruth, and other sport and movie industry icons vie for space with a Presbyterian Church sign, a bicycle, and a wooden yoke. Behind a barber's pole, a piano player bangs out a tune. A microphone is handed to anyone in the crowd who wants to sing along. Furthermore, Lutes Casino is not a casino at all.

In the early 1900s, a general store occupied the building on Main Street. Soon after, a billiards and beer parlor took its place. When the Lutes family took over the business, they added dominos and hamburgers to the pool hall mix. Around 1960, Bob Lutes began to display other people's junk as entertaining treasures. He happily passes out souvenir key chains that say, "I said No to Bob."

The casino's clientele is as eclectic as the décor. Winter Yumans, escaping their colder climate up north, blend right in with local politicians and pool-playing cowboys.

SIRLOIN POTATO PACKETS

1 potato, peeled and thinly sliced

Two 1-lb (450 g) top sirloin steaks

3 Tbsp (45 mL) Worcestershire sauce

2 tsp (10 mL) dried tarragon leaves

¾ tsp (4 mL) ground allspice

¾ tsp (4 mL) garlic powder

1 cup (250 mL) finely chopped mild onion

12 thin slices Monterey Jack cheese

10 strips of bacon

PLACE THE POTATO slices in a microwaveable container. Cover potatoes with water. Cook on high for 1–2 minutes or until tender but not soft. Drain and set aside to cool.

Trim sinew from the steaks. Pound the steaks to an even thickness between ¼–½ inch (0.6–1 cm).

In a bowl, combine the Worcestershire sauce, tarragon, allspice, and garlic powder. Brush the mixture over the surface of the steaks.

Divide the onion, cheese, and potato slices into 4 equal portions.

Spread one portion of the chopped onion in the middle of each steak leaving an equal distance on each end of the meat uncovered for overlapping. Cover the onion with one portion of the cheese and one portion of the potato slices.

Fold one end of each steak over the potato slices to create a new layer. Brush the top of the new layers with the marinade mixture. Place one portion of the onion, cheese, and potato slices over the marinade on each steak.

Fold the remaining end of the steaks over the potatoes to form a packet. For each steak packet, place 3 strips of bacon side by side on a cutting board. Lay 2 strips of bacon perpendicular on top of the first 3 strips. Place the sirloin packets on the centers of the bacon strips. Fold the bacon tightly over the packets. Secure the bacon ends with toothpicks.

Preheat the grill on high (550–600°F/290–315°C) for 10 minutes with the lid closed. Using a pair of long-handled tongs, oil the grate by wiping it with a piece of folded paper towel dipped lightly in canola oil.

Turn one side of the grill off and leave the other side on medium to maintain a temperature of about 375–400°F (190–200°C).

Place the meat on the unlit side of the grate. Cook for 1–1¼ hours or until the internal temperature registers 150–160°F (66–71°C) on an instant-read thermometer.

Remove the sirloin potato packets from the grill. Let the meat rest for 10 minutes before slicing.

Following the Food Truck Frenzy

A FOOD TRUCK festival is like a buffet. We are pulled in every direction by the graphics on the trucks, the aromas in the air. The longest lines indicate the best food. We have to plan our strategy. We go our separate ways to meet up later and examine each other's choices. Sometimes we share. The names of the trucks are enough to make anyone hungry. Brazen Sandwich. Make Me Melt. Thai-U-Up. Pig Rig. Knockout Taco. Shrimp Shack. Cupcake Frolic.

Our food truck experiences, in the past, have been serendipitous. Now, by checking Facebook and Twitter, we can track the whereabouts of these gourmet street vendors at any given moment, no matter what city in North America we happen to be visiting.

We have stood in line in the desert in Phoenix, Arizona, under the lights at night in Apopka, Florida, under the hot afternoon sun in Palm Springs, California, and beside the surf in Punalu'u, Hawaii. The Tampa Bay Food Truck Rally in Tampa, Florida, recently created a new record-breaking count with 99 trucks.

Sidewalk food carts have evolved over the last few years into large, well-equipped, self-propelled kitchens-on-wheels that present an array of ethnic and fusion cuisine. These trucks offer opportunity for first-time entrepreneurs as well as street-level exposure for well-known chefs.

LOCO MOCO

¼ cup (60 mL) butter, divided

¼ cup (60 mL) diced onions

4 cups (1 L) beef broth

2 Tbsp (30 mL) cornstarch

4 tsp (20 mL) water

Four 4-oz (110 g) ground beef patties

2–3 cups (500–750 mL) cooked rice

4 eggs

¼ cup (60 mL) chopped green onions

IN A SAUCEPAN, melt 2 Tbsp (15 mL) butter. Add the onions. Stir and cook until the onions are tender. Add the beef broth to the saucepan and cook for 5 minutes over medium heat.

In a small bowl, mix the cornstarch with the water. Stir the mixture into the beef broth.

Cook and stir until the gravy is thickened.

Preheat the grill on high (550–600°F/290–315°C) for 10 minutes with the lid closed. Using a pair of long-handled tongs, oil the grate by wiping it with a piece of folded paper towel dipped lightly in canola oil.

Reduce the heat to medium-high (450–550°F/230–290°C).

Grill the patties for 5 minutes on each side with the lid closed or until the internal temperature registers 160°F (71°C) on an instant-read thermometer.

In a frying pan, melt remaining butter over medium heat. Fry the eggs to desired doneness, or approximately 2–3 minutes for sunny side up as in most Loco Moco dishes.

Divide the cooked rice between 4 individual plates. On each plate, place a beef patty on top of the rice. Pour gravy over the beef patty and the rice. Top everything with the fried egg. Garnish with the green onions. Serve immediately.

Cartoon Character Not So Cute

IN THE DESERT, where the days are hot and the nights are cool, most critters are the same brown and grey as the landscape. Roadrunners are no exception. They blend right in. And they would go unnoticed if it weren't for their strange behavior. Like its cartoon counterpart, the bird is entertaining and cute in a unique sort of way.

A roadrunner looks a lot like a scrawny chicken, but it has a tail the length of its body. Strutting with a long beak and a jagged crest of feathers, it prefers walking and running to flying. Short, rounded wings can't keep the bird's body airborne for more than a few seconds.

In its desert home, a roadrunner eats scorpions, lizards, and rodents—and rattlesnakes. Not wanting to stumble upon one of these slithering creatures ourselves, we appreciate this.

However, we have learned that a tiny hummingbird is like an hors d'oeuvre in the roadrunner's diet. This is where we draw the line. Any creature that jumps up and catches a hummingbird, midair, is no longer cute.

Occasionally, a roadrunner would approach our motor home door, like a nosey neighbor, looking for food. Some people cooked hamburger for their feathered visitors. They would even make special little meatballs for them. When their roadrunner guests appeared, they would pop the meatballs in the microwave for a few seconds before serving. No wonder the roadrunners returned to their door day after day.

Our Cast Iron Sweet & Sour Meatballs (see next page) are not for roadrunners.

CAST IRON SWEET & SOUR MEATBALLS

20–24 pre-cooked, frozen meatballs	½ cup (125 mL) water	1 Tbsp (15 mL) soy sauce
¼ cup (60 mL) white vinegar	½ cup (125 mL) brown sugar	½ tsp (2 mL) hot sauce
½ cup (125 mL) ketchup	2 Tbsp (30 mL) cornstarch	Canola oil (for brushing)

DEFROST THE MEATBALLS overnight in the refrigerator.

In a bowl, combine the remaining ingredients. Mix well. Set aside.

Thread the meatballs onto skewers. Brush the meatballs lightly with canola oil. Set aside.

Preheat the grill on medium-high (450–550°F/230–290°C) for 10 minutes with the lid closed. Using a pair of long-handled tongs, oil the grate by wiping it with a piece of folded paper towel dipped lightly in canola oil.

Place the meatball skewers on one side of the grate. Place the cast iron frying pan on the other side of the grate.

Pour the sweet and sour sauce into the frying pan. With a long handled spoon, constantly stir the sweet and sour sauce until the sauce thickens.

While the sauce is cooking, grill the meatballs, with the lid open, for 2 minutes per side or until browned and hot.

Push the meatballs off the skewers and into the sauce. Gently stir and cook for about 10 minutes.

Use heavy-duty oven mitts to remove the cast iron pan from the grill.

Cattle Roundup in Cowtown

CATTLE DRIVES WERE commonplace in the 1880s, when cowboys on horses moved herds of cattle across counties and states. Today, cattle drives live on in Fort Worth, Texas. Twice a day, real cowboys run cattle along Exchange Avenue in the Stockyards National Historic District. Texas longhorns shuffle down the street, heads bobbing, horns long and pointy, while cowboys follow on horseback with their lassos ready for the steer that decides to take a different path. The cattle drive celebrates a long-lasting cowboy tradition from the days when Fort Worth was known as Cowtown.

With the arrival of the railroad, Fort Worth became the hub of the cattle industry. Where saloons, hotels, and shopkeepers originally offered cowboys rest, relaxation, and supplies for the upcoming cattle drive, massive facilities were constructed for the purchase, sale, and slaughter of cattle, sheep, and hogs. As the prospects of the stockyards declined in the last half of the twentieth century after years of prosperity, the Fort Worth Stockyards National District was created to preserve historical landmarks.

The stockyards in Fort Worth, the last standing stockyards in the United States, have become a tourist destination. Visitors can whoop it up in honky-tonk saloons, test their directional skills in a maze of cattle pens, witness a shootout, cheer bull riders at a rodeo, or visit the Texas Cowboy Museum. Shops and pubs depict the Cowtown image.

SMOKED BEEF BRISKET

6 lb (2.7 kg) beef brisket

Canola oil (for rubbing on the brisket)

¼ cup (60 mL) sea salt

2 Tbsp (30 mL) coarsely ground pepper

1 Tbsp (15 mL) garlic powder

1 tsp (5 mL) cayenne pepper

1 cup (250 mL) beef broth

1 Tbsp (15 mL) apple cider vinegar

2 Tbsp (30 mL) brown sugar

1 tsp (5 mL) pepper

LEAVING A ¼-inch (6 mm) thick layer of fat on the top, trim excess exterior fat from the brisket. Rinse the meat and pat dry with paper towels.

Place the brisket in a large bowl or roasting pan. Rub canola oil over the entire brisket.

Combine the salt, pepper, garlic powder, and cayenne in a bowl to create a rub.

Massage the rub into the meat. Cover tightly and refrigerate for 8–12 hours.

Preheat the smoker to medium-low (225°F/105°C). Place the brisket on the grate, fat-side up. Cook for 4 hours or until the internal temperature of the meat registers 150°F (66°C) on an instant-read thermometer. Turn the brisket over halfway through the cooking time.

Remove the brisket from the smoker. Do not turn off the smoker.

Set the brisket on a large, double layer of heavy-duty aluminum foil. Create a foil bowl around the meat. Pour the beef broth into the bowl. Wrap the brisket and liquid tightly with the foil.

Return the foil-wrapped roast to the smoker and continue cooking at 225°F (105°C) for 2½ hours or until the internal temperature registers 200°F (95°C) on an instant-read thermometer.

Transfer the brisket to a roasting pan to rest for 30 minutes. Do not remove the foil from the brisket. Cover the pan tightly. Save the broth by removing the foil from the brisket while still in the roasting pan.

In a saucepan, over medium heat, combine the saved broth with the cider vinegar, brown sugar, and pepper. Stir until the sugar dissolves and the broth is hot.

Just before serving, slice the brisket the thickness of a pencil, against the grain. Do not slice until ready to serve, to prevent drying out. Place the slices on a platter and drizzle with the broth.

Refrigerate leftover brisket and slice thinly against the grain for sandwiches.

POULTRY

Down on the Farm in Key West

IN KEY WEST, Florida, each day begins with an unharmonious announcement by a chorus of roosters. The sound is akin to a group of brass band musicians warming their instruments prior to a performance. There is no rest for visitors who want to sleep until dawn when these red-crowned alarm clocks begin their incessant cock-a-doodle-doos as early as 4:30 a.m. It's like waking up on the farm.

During the day, these roosters and their feathered families are everywhere. Some outdoor cafes have more poultry strutting their stuff under the tables than on the menu. As cute as mother hens and baby chicks appear in the bright Florida sun, in the early hours before dawn we dream of grilling them and serving them on platters garnished with fresh Florida oranges.

In comparison, sunsets on the Keys are subdued and quiet. While standing with hundreds of others at Mallory Square, anticipation-filled chatter gives way to sudden respectful silence as the flaming ball spreads its color across the Gulf of Mexico and slips below the horizon. The air is instantly cooler. Yawns become hard to suppress. After all, we have been awake since dawn. The roosters are already asleep, perched in trees, shrubs, and on rooftops, resting their vocal cords in preparation for a new day.

Our Hot Orange Chicken Drumsticks recipe (see next page) combines all the attributes of Key West: citrus, heat, and of course, chicken.

HOT ORANGE CHICKEN DRUMSTICKS

10–12 chicken drumsticks	2 Tbsp (30 mL) hot sauce, divided	3 Tbsp (45 mL) orange marmalade
½ cup (125 mL) orange juice	2 Tbsp (30 mL) extra-virgin olive oil	1 orange, sliced for garnish

TRIM THE DRUMSTICKS of any excess fat and place them in a bowl.

In a separate bowl, combine the orange juice, 1 Tbsp (15 mL) hot sauce, and oil. Mix well.

Pour the orange juice marinade into a resealable plastic bag. Add the drumsticks and seal the bag tightly. Massage the bag gently to coat the drumsticks with the orange mixture. Place the bag in the refrigerator on a flat plate for 8–12 hours. Turn bag over once or twice while marinating.

In a bowl, combine the orange marmalade with the remaining hot sauce. Set aside.

Preheat the grill on high (550–600°F/290–315°C) for 10 minutes with the lid closed. Using a pair of long-handled tongs, oil the grate by wiping it with a piece of folded paper towel dipped lightly in canola oil. Reduce the heat to low (250–300°F/120–175°C).

Remove drumsticks from the marinade. Discard the marinade.

Place the drumsticks on the grate. Brush them with the marmalade mixture. Close the lid.

Grill the drumsticks for a total of 30–35 minutes, turning every 8–10 minutes and brushing with the marmalade mixture. Transfer the drumsticks to a serving plate when the internal temperature of the meat registers 180°F (82°C) on an instant-read thermometer.

Garnish with orange slices.

HONEY-LEMON HERBED CHICKEN HALVES

4–6 sprigs of any combination of fresh sage, tarragon, thyme, or rosemary

5–6 lb (2.2–2.7 kg) whole chicken

2 Tbsp (30 mL) extra-virgin olive oil

¼ cup (60 mL) fresh lemon juice

2 Tbsp (30 mL) honey

2 tsp (10 mL) garlic powder

1 tsp (5 mL) sea salt

1 tsp (5 mL) coarsely ground pepper

1 lemon, cut in half

Canola oil (for brushing)

PLACE THE HERB sprigs in a bowl of water.

Rinse the chicken inside and out. Trim away excess fat around the cavity opening. Pat chicken dry with paper towels. Place the chicken, breast-side down, on a large cutting board.

With kitchen scissors, cut all the way along both sides of the backbone, from tail to neck. Remove the backbone.

Turn the chicken breast-side up. Cut along one side of the breastbone from the tail to neck to separate the two halves of the chicken.

Preheat the grill on medium (350–450°F/175–230°C) for 10 minutes with the lid closed. Using a pair of long-handled tongs, oil the grate by wiping it with a piece of folded paper towel dipped lightly in canola oil.

Turn one side of the grill off and leave the other side on medium heat to maintain a temperature of about 350°F (175°C).

In a bowl, combine the oil, lemon juice, honey, garlic powder, salt, and pepper.

Brush each half chicken with the lemon mixture.

Remove the herbs from the water and place them on the unlit portion of the grate.

Place the chicken halves, breast-side up, on top of the herbs.

Close the lid and cook for 1¼–1½ hours, basting with the lemon mixture every 30 minutes. Rotate the chicken if one side is browning too quickly.

When the internal temperature of the breast registers 170°F (77°C) and the thigh registers 180°F (82°C) on an instant-read thermometer, transfer the chicken to the hot side of the grill. Turn the chicken breast-side down and grill, with the lid closed, for about 10 minutes to crisp the skin. Turn the chicken breast-side up and grill for 5 minutes over the direct heat. Discard the herbs.

Oil the cut side of the lemon halves and place them, cut-side down, on the hot grate for about 5 minutes or until lightly charred.

Transfer the chicken halves to a platter. Squeeze the charred lemon over the chicken before cutting into portions.

SPEARED CHICKEN

Four 6–8 oz (170–230 g) boneless, skinless chicken breasts

3 Tbsp (45 mL) fresh lemon juice

¼ tsp (1 mL) dried thyme leaves, crumbled

¼ tsp (1 mL) dried rosemary leaves, crumbled

¼ tsp (1 mL) dried oregano leaves

¼ tsp (1 mL) salt

¼ tsp (1 mL) pepper

¼ cup (60 mL) extra-virgin olive oil

CUT THE CHICKEN breasts into 1-inch (2.5 cm) cubes.

In a medium bowl, combine the lemon juice, thyme, rosemary, oregano, salt, and pepper. Slowly stir the olive oil into the bowl.

Place the marinade in a resealable plastic bag. Add the chicken cubes. Seal the bag tightly and shake the bag to completely coat the chicken. Place the bag flat on a plate in the refrigerator. Marinate for 2–3 hours.

Thread the chicken cubes onto metal or wooden skewers with space between the pieces to ensure the chicken cooks evenly. If using wooden skewers, soak them for 30 minutes in water before using.

Preheat the barbecue on medium (350–450°F/175–230°C) for 10 minutes with the lid closed. Using a pair of long-handled tongs, oil the grate by wiping it with a piece of folded paper towel dipped lightly in canola oil.

Cook the chicken with the lid closed for 4–6 minutes on each side or until the chicken is cooked through.

Along the North Alabama Barbecue Trail

BARBECUE IS SERIOUS business in North Alabama. For four generations, Big Bob Gibson Bar-B-Q in Decatur, Alabama, has been producing championship-level barbecue. It all began with a backyard hand-dug pit. The restaurant competes annually against over 250 teams in the granddaddy of barbecue competitions, the World Championship Barbecue Cooking Contest, part of the month-long Memphis in May international festival of music and food in Memphis, Tennessee.

Back at the restaurant in Decatur, almost an entire page of Big Bob Gibson's menu is dedicated to its list of awards for lip-smacking sauces and down-home cooking. As we stepped in the front door, a smokey, semi-sweet aroma wafted from an old-style brick-lined barbecue pit set up in the back corner of the kitchen.

Over in Athens, Alabama, LawLer's Barbecue takes slow-cooked hand-pulled meats and serves them up fast. Old-time family recipes are prepared at a commissary, then served from shiny stainless steel equipment in several locations. Drive-through windows allow people on the run to enjoy the same delicious food as the people dining inside.

According to Jim Kelley, co-owner of LawLer's, the magic that sets one pit master above another is the amount of love put into the process. With this in mind, there is a lot of love for barbecue in North Alabama. So much so that there is a free app that follows the North Alabama Barbecue Trail.

White barbecue sauce is the most popular sauce in North Alabama, where it was created. Drizzled over chicken, the combination of flavors is nothing but love.

CHICKEN BREASTS WITH NORTH ALABAMA WHITE BARBECUE SAUCE

Four 6–8 oz (170–230 g) large chicken breasts, bone in, skin on

¼ cup (60 mL) melted butter

2 tsp (10 mL) extra-virgin olive oil

½ Tbsp (7.5 mL) garlic powder

1 tsp (5 mL) seasoned salt

1½ cups (375 mL) North Alabama White Barbecue Sauce (recipe follows)

PREHEAT THE GRILL on high (550–600°F/290–315°C) for 10 minutes with the lid closed. Using a pair of long-handled tongs, oil the grate by wiping it with a piece of folded paper towel dipped lightly in canola oil.

In a bowl, combine the butter, oil, garlic powder, and seasoned salt. Mix well.

Brush the chicken breasts with half the butter mixture. Save the rest for basting the chicken.

Turn one side of the grill off and leave the other side on medium-high heat (450–550°F/230–290°C) to maintain a temperature of about 400°F (200°C).

Place the chicken, skin-side down, on the hot side of the grill for 8 minutes with the lid closed.

Turn the breasts over, brush the skin with the remaining butter mixture, and cook for 10 minutes.

Transfer the chicken, skin-side up, to the unlit side of the grate. Cook, lid closed, for 10 minutes or until the internal temperature registers 170°F (77°C) on an instant-read thermometer.

Transfer the chicken breasts to a platter. Drizzle North Alabama White Barbecue Sauce over top. Serve extra sauce on the side.

NORTH ALABAMA WHITE BARBECUE SAUCE

1 cup (250 mL) mayonnaise

6 Tbsp (90 mL) white vinegar

½ tsp (2 mL) fresh lemon juice

1 Tbsp (15 mL) white sugar

½ tsp (2 mL) coarsely ground pepper

½ tsp (2 mL) sea salt

⅛ tsp (0.5 mL) garlic powder

⅛ tsp (0.5 mL) onion powder

IN A BOWL, combine all ingredients.

Cover and refrigerate until ready to use.

This sauce can be stored in a sealed container in the refrigerator for 3 days.

SAVORY CHICKEN BREASTS

¼ cup (60 mL) extra-virgin olive oil

2 Tbsp (30 mL) fresh lemon juice

3 Tbsp (45 mL) red wine vinegar

2 Tbsp (30 mL) corn syrup

½ tsp (2 mL) paprika

1 tsp (5 mL) dried basil leaves

Four to six 6–8 oz (170–230 g) boneless, skinless chicken breasts

IN A BOWL, combine all ingredients but the chicken breasts. Stir well.

Trim the chicken breasts and place them in a resealable plastic bag. Pour the marinade over the chicken. Seal the bag tightly. Shake the bag to coat the chicken with marinade. Place the bag on a plate. Refrigerate for 6–8 hours. Turn the bag over at least once while the chicken marinates.

Remove the chicken breasts from the bag and discard the marinade.

Preheat the grill on medium-high (450–550°F/230–290°C) for 10 minutes with the lid closed. Turn the heat down to medium (350–450°F/175–230°C). Using a pair of long-handled tongs, oil the grate by wiping it with a piece of folded paper towel dipped lightly in canola oil.

Grill the chicken breasts with the lid closed for 8–10 minutes on each side, or until the juices run clear and the internal temperature registers 170°F (77°C) on an instant-read thermometer.

GRANOLA CRUSTED CHICKEN

¼ cup (60 mL) liquid honey

¼ cup (60 mL) lemon juice

3 cups (750 mL) granola cereal

Four 6-8 oz (170-230 g) boneless, skinless chicken breasts

IN A SMALL bowl, combine the honey and lemon juice. Set aside.

Chop the cereal into fine pieces in a food processor or crush in a tightly sealed plastic bag with a rolling pin. Place the crushed granola in a flat baking dish. Set aside.

Trim excess fat from the chicken breasts. Cut the breasts into strips about 1 inch (2.5 cm) wide.

Place a grill topper on the grate. Preheat the grill on high (550–600°F/290–315°C) for 10 minutes with the lid closed. Using a pair of long-handled tongs, oil the grill topper by wiping it with a piece of folded paper towel dipped lightly in canola oil.

Reduce the temperature to medium (350–450°F/175–230°C). Place the chicken strips on the grill topper.

Grill and turn with the lid closed for about 8 minutes or until the chicken is golden brown on both sides and cooked through.

Remove the chicken from the grill and brush thoroughly with the honey lemon mixture.

Roll the tenders in the crushed granola until they are coated with the cereal.

Lou Ah Vull, Kentucky

LOUISVILLE, KENTUCKY—LOU-AH-VULL to the locals— is packed with cultural, sport, and food surprises. Museums, arts centers, and sports history share the downtown stage.

Mohammed Ali was born and raised in Louisville. Films and memorabilia in the Mohammed Ali Center tell his story—from childhood to captivating international spokesman. The Louisville Slugger Museum and Factory is home to the world's largest baseball bat. The 120-foot (36.5 meter) tall, 68,000-lb (30,844 kg) steel bat that lures photographers, baseball fans, and visitors to Main Street and Museum Row. The gargantuan bat is a replica of Babe Ruth's 34-inch (86 cm) Louisville Slugger.

Louisville Stoneware, a company that transforms clay into versatile, functional art celebrated a 200th anniversary in 2015. Louisville is also the home of the Kentucky Derby, the race of thoroughbred horses that has run every consecutive year since 1875. The mint julep cocktail is a Derby tradition, as are the ladies' elaborate hats.

In 1926, another tradition began in the city when the chef at the Louisville Brown Hotel created an alternative to ham and eggs for the hotel's hungry late-night revelers. The new creation was an open-faced turkey sandwich smothered with a rich cheese sauce, sprinkled with Parmesan, oven-broiled, and topped with bacon and pimento. The sandwich became known as the Hot Brown.

The Hot Brown is so popular that most restaurants in Louisville and outlying areas put a twist on the original recipe. Menus offer variations like the Brown Derby, the Hot Brown Florentine, the Seafood Hot Brown and the Baby Hot Brown.

Our version of the Hot Brown (see next page) includes brined turkey breast and comes with a warning: portions are generous, and there may not be room for dessert.

HOT BROWN WITH BRINED TURKEY BREAST

FOR THE BRINED TURKEY

2–2½ lb (0.9–1.2 kg) turkey breast,
bone in, skin on

4 cups (1 L) Poultry Brine
(see page 233)

¼ cup (60 mL) brown sugar

2 tsp (10 mL) coarsely ground pepper

1 tsp (5 mL) ground ginger

½ tsp (2 mL) dried rosemary leaves,
crumbled

Olive oil (for brushing)

FOR THE SANDWICH

¼ cup (60 mL) butter

⅓ cup (80 mL) all-purpose flour

At least 6 cups (1.5 L) milk

¼ tsp (1 mL) white pepper

3 cups (750 mL) grated mild cheddar
cheese

6 large slices sourdough bread

1½ lb (700 g) thin slices of the brined
turkey breast (see above)

16 slices crisp cooked bacon,
chopped small

3 medium fresh tomatoes,
chopped small

1½ cups (375 mL) shredded
Parmesan cheese

PLACE THE TURKEY breast in a large resealable plastic bag. Carefully pour the poultry brine into the bag. Seal the bag tightly. Place the bag on a flat dish in the refrigerator for 24 hours.

In a bowl, combine the brown sugar, pepper, ginger, and rosemary. Mix well. Set aside.

Remove the turkey breast from the brine. Rinse under cold water and pat dry with paper towels.

Place the turkey breast in a large dish and lightly brush olive oil over the breast. Pat the brown sugar mixture over the entire breast. Refrigerate for 30 minutes.

Preheat the grill on high (550–600°F/290–315°C) for 10 minutes with the lid closed. Using a pair of long-handled tongs, oil the grate by wiping it with a piece of paper towel dipped lightly in canola oil.

Prepare the grill for indirect cooking. Turn one side of the grill off and leave the other side on medium-high (450–550°F/230–290°C) heat to maintain a temperature of 375–400°F (190–200°C).

Place the turkey breast, skin-side up, on the unlit side of the grate.

Cook, with the lid closed, for 1¼–1½ hours or until the internal temperature registers 170°F (77°C) on an instant-read thermometer. Rotate the turkey breast on the grate halfway through the cooking time.

RECIPE CONTINUED…

Transfer the turkey breast to a cutting board. Cover with aluminum foil and let stand for 10 minutes before slicing or cover with plastic wrap and refrigerate overnight.

To make the hot brown sandwich, melt the butter in a saucepan over medium heat. Remove from heat and stir in the flour, whisking constantly until smooth. Continue to whisk while slowly adding the milk. Place the saucepan back over medium heat. Whisk constantly until the sauce is thickened and the flour is cooked.

Stir in the white pepper and grated cheddar cheese. Stir until the cheese is completely melted.

If the cheese sauce needs to be thinned, add extra milk 2 Tbsp (30 mL) at a time.

Toast the sourdough bread.

Slice the turkey and divide the slices evenly over the slices of toast.

Spoon the cheese sauce over the sliced turkey. Top the cheese sauce with the chopped bacon and chopped tomatoes. Sprinkle the Parmesan cheese over the bacon and tomato.

SMOKED TURKEY LEGS

½ cup (125 mL) chicken broth

¼ cup (60 mL) maple syrup

1 Tbsp (15 mL) lemon juice

4–6 medium-sized turkey legs

1 Tbsp (15 mL) brown sugar

1 tsp (5 mL) smoked paprika

½ tsp (2 mL) garlic powder

¼ tsp (1 mL) coarsely ground pepper

IN A BOWL, mix the liquid ingredients.

Siphon the liquid into an injector needle (kitchen syringe) and inject each turkey leg 3–4 times.

In a bowl, combine the dry ingredients.

Set the turkey legs, drum end up, in a tall, narrow bowl to prevent injected liquid from running out.

Pat the brown sugar mixture over the legs.

Preheat the smoker to medium-low (225°F/105°C).

Place the turkey legs directly on the grate. Close the lid and cook for about 3–4 hours or until the internal temperature registers 170°F (77°C) on an instant-read thermometer. Timing will depend on the size of the turkey legs.

They Knew We Were Coming

EAGLE PLAINS, YUKON, is the halfway mark on the Dempster Highway that runs from the Yukon Territory to Inuvik, Northwest Territories, in Canada's far north. Surrounded by frozen tundra, the Eagle Plains Hotel was built on a natural pad of solid bedrock in 1978, just before the completion of the Dempster Highway. It is the only stop for gas, food, and lodging along the 426-mile (685 kilometer) gravel road that winds its way through the land of the Gwich'in people to the land of the Inuvialuit in Inuvik, the gateway to the Western Arctic.

When we finally reached Eagle Plains and pulled up to the pumps for gas, the service man said they had been expecting us—for several days. Locals who had passed us along the route and drive the highway regularly had reported our progress. Our pace up the Dempster was purposely slow. There was so much to see.

The Dempster Highway is named after Inspector Dempster, an outstanding dog musher who made a grueling drive with his sled and team to determine the fate of the Lost Patrol, four members of the Northwest Mounted Police who perished on the trail in the winter of 1910–1911.

Photos inside the Eagle Plains Hotel tell the story of Albert Johnson, the Mad Trapper of Rat River. Involved in tampering with First Nations traplines, Johnson killed one mounted policeman and wounded another. He eluded the Mounties for 48 days before being killed in a shootout.

North of Eagle Plains, low bush cranberries grow over the rocks at the Arctic Circle. A delicacy, they would add an element of natural flavor to any recipe.

TURKEY CRANBERRY KABOBS

¼ cup (60 mL) canola oil

1 small garlic clove, finely chopped

¾ tsp (4 mL) dried sage leaves

¼ tsp (1 mL) salt

¼ tsp (1 mL) pepper

1–1½ lb (450–700 g) skinless, boneless turkey breasts

½–¾ cup (125–185 mL) dried cranberries

COMBINE THE OIL, garlic, sage, salt, and pepper in a bowl. Mix well. Set aside.

Cut the turkey breast into 1-inch (2.5 cm) cubes.

Thread the turkey cubes onto metal or wooden skewers, putting 2 or 3 dried cranberries between each turkey cube. If using wooden skewers, soak them for 30 minutes in water before using.

Preheat the grill on medium (350–450°F/175–230°C) for 10 minutes with the lid closed. Using a pair of long-handled tongs, oil the grate by wiping it with a piece of folded paper towel dipped lightly in canola oil.

Grill the kabobs with the lid closed for 5–6 minutes on each side or until the turkey is cooked through. Brush the garlic-sage mixture on the kabobs every 2–3 minutes.

Serve immediately.

The March of the Peabody Ducks

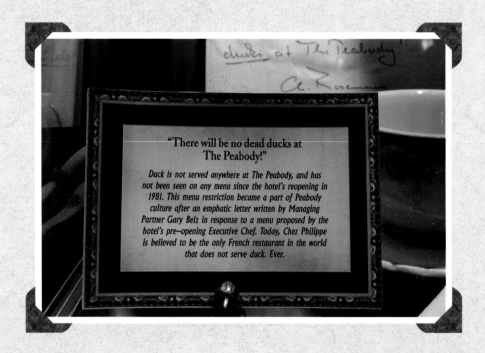

> "There will be no dead ducks at The Peabody!"
>
> *Duck is not served anywhere at The Peabody, and has not been seen on any menu since the hotel's reopening in 1981. This menu restriction became a part of Peabody culture after an emphatic letter written by Managing Partner Gary Belz in response to a menu proposed by the hotel's pre-opening Executive Chef. Today, Chez Philippe is believed to be the only French restaurant in the world that does not serve duck. Ever.*

EVERY DAY, THE Peabody Ducks leave their private palace on the roof of the Peabody Memphis, a hotel in Memphis, Tennessee, to waddle into an elevator, descend to the main floor, and parade along a red carpet to the hotel's grand fountain under the tutelage of the hotel's Duckmaster. The Duckmaster is in charge of everything duck-related.

The March of the Peabody Ducks began in the 1930s when the general manager of the hotel was also a duck hunter. Live duck decoys were legal at the time. Jack Daniels was not legal, but the manager and his friends took the Tennessee whiskey along on their hunting trips. Returning to the hotel after one particular outing, the manager neglected to leave his live decoys at the farm where they belonged. Under the influence of Jack Daniels, he placed the ducks in the hotel fountain, an ornate Italian marble art piece.

In the morning, the general manager rushed down to the lobby to find the ducks still paddling contentedly in the fountain, entertaining hotel guests. A new hotel rule was initiated. As long as guests were enjoying the ducks, the ducks would stay.

The first Duckmaster, a former circus animal trainer, coached his team of water birds to parade to the fountain to the tune of John Philip Sousa's "King Cotton March." The tradition continues over 80 years later.

At precisely 11:00 a.m., we watched five North American mallards march and quack out of the elevator to the fountain. Every day at 5 p.m., the performers return to their rooftop palace.

To this day, there is no duck served on any menu in the Peabody Memphis.

SMOKED HONEY-ORANGE DUCK

4–5 lb (1.8–2.2 kg) duck

2 Tbsp (30 mL) sesame oil

1 orange, cut into quarters

1–2 sprigs of fresh rosemary

¼ cup (60 mL) brown sugar

1 tsp (5 mL) garlic powder

1 tsp (5 mL) ginger powder

¼ tsp (1 mL) sea salt

¼ tsp (1 mL) coarsely ground pepper

3 Tbsp (45 mL) liquid honey

1 Tbsp (15 mL) orange juice

1 Tbsp (15 mL) hoisin sauce

TRIM EXCESS FAT from the duck cavities and cut off the wing tips.

Rinse the duck inside and out. Dry inside and out with paper towels. Place the duck, breast-side up, in a large non-metallic dish.

Using a fondue fork or the sharp point of a paring knife, poke small holes in the skin of the breast and thighs, on an angle without puncturing the meat.

Rub the duck lightly with sesame oil. Place the orange pieces and the fresh rosemary inside the duck.

In a bowl, combine the dry ingredients. Pat the dry mixture over the breast and legs of the duck.

Cover the dish with plastic wrap and refrigerate for 2–4 hours.

In a bowl, combine the remaining ingredients. Set aside.

Preheat the smoker to medium-high (325°F/160°C) with apple or cherry wood.

Set the duck on the grate breast side up.

With the lid closed, cook for about 2–2½ hours or until the internal temperature at the leg joint registers 175°F (80°C) on an instant-read thermometer and the legs move freely. Brush the duck breast and legs with the honey mixture every 40 minutes. At the same time, prick the skin.

A drip pan under the duck may be necessary to control the fat runoff.

For a crispier skin, turn the smoker up to high heat during the last 10–15 minutes.

Transfer the cooked duck to a platter and cover with a loose tent of aluminum foil for 15 minutes before carving.

SEAFOOD

Low Tide at Halls Harbour

AS WE DROVE past fishing boats on our way to the Lobster Pound in Halls Harbour, Nova Scotia, we noticed that the boats were sitting on the harbor's muddy bottom. Floating docks leaned awkwardly on a waterless bank. Only a tiny stream of water, mid-harbor, flowed out to sea. This is what happens at low tide in the Bay of Fundy.

Over 100 billion tons of water move in and out of the Bay twice every 24 hours. This volume is equal to the daily discharge of all the world's rivers. Along Nova Scotia's Atlantic Coast, the tidal range is 5–8 feet (1.5–2.5 meters). The tidal measurements in the Midas Basin, on the Halls Harbour side of the province, at the Head of the Bay of Fundy, are the highest recorded in the world, at 52 feet (16 meters). In Halls Harbour, the tide rises as much as 1 inch (2.5 cm) per minute until it reaches the 29-foot (9 meter) high tide mark on the wharf.

We ordered our lobsters from a tank in the gift shop. There was a choice of several sizes. We pointed to two of the largest, weighing in at 2 lb (900 g) each. After paying, we carried the lobsters outside to the cookhouse, a hut filled with steaming tanks of boiling water. We stopped on the way to photograph our catch.

In less than 30 minutes, our lobsters arrived at our picnic table overlooking the harbor. We cracked the shells, pulled out the tender morsels, squeezed lemon juice over the sweet flesh, dipped it in butter, and watched the tide roll in.

For extra flavor, we like to give our lobsters a quick turn on the grill before serving.

BASIC GRILLED WHOLE LOBSTER

¼ cup (60 mL) coarse salt

Four 1–1½ lb (450–700 g)
live lobsters

1 cup (250 mL) salted butter, melted

3 medium garlic cloves,
finely chopped

¼ cup (60 mL) fresh lemon juice

2 lemons cut into wedges (for garnish)

FILL A LARGE pot with enough water to cover the lobsters. Bring the water to a rolling boil and add the salt. Grasp each lobster behind the head and plunge it, head and claws first into the water. Cover the pot.

Begin timing from the moment the water comes back to a boil. Boil the lobsters for 7–8 minutes. Do not overcook.

Transfer the lobsters from the pot to a cutting board.

As soon as the lobsters are cool enough to handle, cut each lobster in half lengthwise with kitchen scissors, cutting the underside first and then the hard upper shell.

Remove and discard the stomach from behind the head and the dark vein running down the back of the tail.

Preheat the grill on medium-high (450–550°F/230–290°C) for 10 minutes with the lid closed. Using a pair of long-handled tongs, oil the grate by wiping it with a piece of folded paper towel dipped lightly in canola oil.

In a bowl, combine the butter, garlic, and lemon juice. Divide the mixture into 2 bowls: one for brushing the lobster before grilling, and the other to use as a condiment when served.

Brush the flesh side of the split lobsters with the butter mixture.

With the lid closed, grill the lobsters, flesh side down, for about 2 minutes or until the flesh is lightly browned.

Turn the lobsters over. Grill, shell-side down, for about 3 minutes with the lid closed.

Serve with lemon wedges and the reserved garlic butter mixture.

LIME BUTTER LOBSTER TAILS

Four 6-oz (170 g) lobster tails

6 Tbsp (90 mL) butter, melted

1 Tbsp (15 mL) fresh lime juice

1 tsp (5 mL) garlic powder

1 Tbsp (15 mL) finely chopped fresh chives

1 Tbsp (15 mL) finely chopped fresh parsley

1 lime cut into wedges (for garnish)

CUT EACH LOBSTER tail in half lengthwise by first cutting each side of the shells with kitchen scissors. Complete the cut through the flesh with a sharp knife.

In a bowl, combine the butter, lime juice, garlic powder, chives, and parsley.

Brush the flesh of the lobster with the lime butter mixture.

Preheat the grill on high (550–600°F/290–315°C) for 10 minutes with the lid closed. Using a pair of long-handled tongs, oil the grate by wiping it with a piece of folded paper towel dipped lightly in canola oil. Reduce the heat to medium (350–450°F/175–230°C).

Place the lobster tails on the hot grate, flesh-side down. Sear the flesh for 2–3 minutes with the lid open.

Turn the tails over, flesh-side up, and grill 4–6 minutes, with the lid closed.

Brush lime butter on the tails as they cook. The lobster tails are cooked when the flesh is white and firm but not dry. Serve with lime wedges.

SUGAR-GLAZED SALMON

| 2 lb (900 g) side of salmon | At least ½ cup (125 mL) mayonnaise | At least ½ cup (125 mL) brown sugar |

PREHEAT THE GRILL on medium-high (450–550°F/230–290°C) for 10 minutes with the lid closed.

On a cutting board, place a double layer of heavy-duty aluminum foil, longer than the length of the salmon. Turn up the edges of the foil to create a lip to prevent juices leaking into the grill.

Brush the top of the aluminum foil lightly with canola oil.

Rinse the salmon with cold water and pat dry with paper towels. Lay the salmon on the foil, skin-side down.

Spread mayonnaise generously over the salmon until the fish is completely covered.

Sprinkle brown sugar generously over the mayonnaise. Gently pat the sugar into the mayonnaise.

Place the salmon and foil onto the preheated grill. Close the lid.

Cook for about 20 minutes or until the internal temperature registers 145°F (63°C) on an instant-read thermometer. The salmon is ready when the flesh is firm but moist, and a golden sugar glaze bubbles on the aluminum foil.

TERIYAKI SALMON TAILS

2 Tbsp (30 mL) chopped ginger

2 cloves garlic, chopped

1 cup (250 mL) sweet apple cider

2 Tbsp (30 mL) soy sauce

Four 6-oz (170 g) salmon tail fillets

IN A SMALL saucepan combine all ingredients but the salmon. Bring the mixture to a boil for 2 minutes. Remove the mixture from the heat. Set aside to cool for about 15 minutes then set in the refrigerator to chill for 15 minutes.

Rinse the salmon fillets and pat dry with paper towel. Place in a shallow dish and pour the ginger marinade over the salmon. Cover with plastic wrap and refrigerate 4–6 hours.

Preheat the grill on high (550–600°F/290–315°C) for 10 minutes with the lid closed. Using a pair of long-handled tongs, oil the grate by wiping it with a piece of folded paper towel dipped lightly in canola oil.

Reduce the heat to medium-high (450–550°F/230–290°C). Place the salmon on the grate, skin-side down. Spoon some of the ginger marinade over the salmon.

Grill the salmon 4–5 minutes with the lid closed.

Turn the salmon over gently with a lifter. Peel away and discard the skin.

Grill the salmon on the second side for about 3–4 minutes or until the salmon is firm but moist.

SALMON GRILLED ON A BED OF ROMAINE

8 romaine lettuce leaves

8 fresh basil leaves

Four 6-oz (170 g) salmon fillets

1–2 lemons, thinly sliced

RINSE THE ROMAINE leaves. Place the leaves in a bowl of water until ready to use.

Rinse the basil. Keep the leaves moist.

Preheat the grill on high (550–600°F/290–315°C) for 10 minutes with the lid closed. Using a pair of long-handled tongs, oil the grate by wiping it with a piece of folded paper towel dipped lightly in canola oil. Reduce the heat to medium (350–450°F/175–230°C).

Transfer the wet romaine leaves from the bowl of water directly to the grate, creating a bed of romaine leaves on the grate. Place the salmon fillets skin-side down on the bed of romaine. Top each fillet with lemon slices and basil leaves.

Grill for approximately 15 minutes with the lid closed or until the romaine leaves are charred and brittle and the salmon is firm but moist.

Discard the romaine.

Tyee Club Tradition

A GROUP OF fishermen in Campbell River, British Columbia, established the Tyee Club of British Columbia in 1924 to assist in the standardization of the sport of salmon fishing. Anglers were returning each year to Campbell River, a community on Vancouver Island, in pursuit of the elusive tyee, also known as the chinook or spring salmon. Membership in the Tyee Club cannot be bought, inherited, or won. It can only be acquired by fishing according to club regulations.

In Campbell River, candidates fish in classic rowboats, without motors. The angler must use a single hook. With the slightest change in the motion of the tip of the rod, the hook must be set, fast and hard, to take on the battle with the Pacific chinook salmon. If the fish is boated and weighs 30 lb (13.5 kg) or more, the catch is recorded and the angler becomes a member of the Tyee Club.

We spent three days in the Thunderbird RV Park in Campbell River at the beginning of the tyee season that runs from mid-July to mid-September. The park is on First Nations land with the Pacific Ocean lapping at the front and the Campbell River flowing at the back. Pods of orca whales visit each year. Historical totem poles are minutes away. In the afternoons, we sat at the ocean's edge with drinks, snacks, binoculars, and cameras. Seaplanes, tug boats, cruise ships, birds, and fishermen in small rowboats kept us entertained.

We caught our salmon at a fish shop located on the dock at the nearby Discovery Bay Marina. A fish may have to be 30 lb (13.5 kg) or more for a fisherman to become a member of the Tyee Club, but any salmon qualifies for our West Coast Cedar Plank Salmon (see next page).

WEST COAST CEDAR PLANK SALMON

3 Tbsp (45 mL) brown sugar

½ Tbsp (7.5 mL) garlic powder

1 tsp (5 mL) Chinese five spice powder

1 tsp (5 mL) hot sauce

3 Tbsp (45 mL) soy sauce

½ Tbsp (45 mL) sesame oil

¼ cup (60 mL) dark molasses

Four 6-oz (170 g) boneless, salmon fillets, skin on

SOAK TWO 12-inch (30 cm) cedar planks in cold water overnight.

In a bowl, combine all ingredients but the salmon. Stir well until blended. The sauce can be made a day or two ahead and refrigerated until ready to use.

Preheat the grill on medium-high (450–550°F/230–290°C) for 10 minutes with the lid closed.

Place the salmon fillets, skin-side down, on the wet cedar planks. Place planks on the hot grate.

Spoon and spread half the brown sugar mixture over the salmon.

Cook the salmon with the lid closed for 15–20 minutes depending on the thickness of the salmon and the thickness of the cedar. The cedar will smoke the fish.

Halfway through cooking, baste the salmon with the remainder of the sauce. Do not turn the salmon over.

Check the cedar planks occasionally. Be prepared to sprinkle baking soda on any flames.

The salmon is cooked when the flesh is firm, but moist. Lift each fillet from the cedar planks, leaving the skin behind.

SHRIMP TACOS WITH MANGO SALSA & FRESH LIME

1 Tbsp (15 mL) lemon juice

1 Tbsp (15 mL) lime juice

1 tsp (5 mL) hot sauce

6 Tbsp (90 mL) canola oil + extra (for brushing)

¼ cup (60 mL) coarsely chopped cilantro

1 garlic clove, finely chopped

¼ tsp (1 mL) ground cumin

¼ tsp (1 mL) sea salt

¼ tsp (1 mL) pepper

24–32 medium raw shrimp, peeled and deveined

2 whole limes, cut in half

8 corn tortillas (5 inch/12 cm)

¾ cup (185 mL) shredded green cabbage

¾ cup (185 mL) Mango Salsa (see page 232)

IN A LARGE glass dish, combine the lemon juice, lime juice, hot sauce, oil, cilantro, garlic, cumin, salt, and pepper. Mix well.

Add the shrimp to the marinade. Stir to coat the shrimp. Cover and refrigerate for 2–4 hours.

Place a grill topper on the grill grate. Preheat the grill on medium-high (450–550°F/230–290°C) for 10 minutes.

Oil the grill topper. Place the shrimp on the grill topper and cook for 2–3 minutes per side or until the shrimp become firm and pink. Do not overcook. Discard the marinade.

Brush the cut side of the limes with canola oil. Place the limes cut side down on the grate and grill until charred, about 2–3 minutes.

Place the tortillas on the grate. Heat each side 20–30 seconds to warm and soften. Remove to a cutting board.

Place 3–4 shrimp along the center of each tortilla. Cover the shrimp with shredded cabbage and the mango salsa.

Serve with the grilled lime halves to squeeze over top.

Eating Our Way Around the Gulf of Mexico

DRIVING WEST TO east around the Gulf of Mexico from Texas to Florida, the warm water of the Gulf was never far from sight—and the seafood selection was seductive.

On South Padre Island, Texas, we squeezed fresh lemon over chargrilled amberjack and grouper. On our way up the Texas coast, we purchased shrimp fresh off the boats.

In Louisiana, we ate gumbo that was rich, dark brown, and loaded with andouille sausage and Gulf shrimp. A crawfish boil in Scott, Louisiana, was followed by fried soft shell crab in Biloxi, Mississippi.

Along the white, sandy beaches of Gulf Shores and Orange Beach, Alabama, we lingered over peel-and-eat royal red shrimp and the best buttery, sweet, raw oysters. We were introduced to lionfish, sheepshead, and hog snapper by the NUISANCE Group, an organization that puts underutilized or invasive fish into the kitchens of creative restaurant chefs and home cooks.

In Panama City Beach, Florida, we ate steamed Apalachicola oysters with lemon juice and a dash of Tabasco. Heading down Florida's west coast, at a picnic table near Sarasota, in-house smoked mackerel and stone crab claws were hors d'oeuvres to a feast of broiled red snapper.

As we immersed ourselves in the diversity of seafood along the Gulf of Mexico, no matter what our location, shrimp were always on the menu—royal reds, whites, pinks, and even browns. We enjoyed them grilled, broiled, sautéed, and skewered. The citrus shrimp in our Citrus Shrimp Kabobs (see next page) captures the essence of our journey.

CITRUS SHRIMP KABOBS

2 Tbsp (30 mL) lemon juice

2 Tbsp (30 mL) orange juice

2 Tbsp (30 mL) extra-virgin olive oil

1 tsp (5 mL) coarsely chopped
fresh thyme

½ tsp (2 mL) garlic powder

½ tsp (2 mL) seasoned salt

24 large shrimp, peeled
and deveined

4 lemon wedges

4 orange wedges

IN A SMALL bowl, combine all ingredients but the shrimp and fruit wedges.

Use 2 metal or wooden skewers for each shrimp kabob. (If using wooden skewers, soak for 30 minutes in water first.) Thread the first skewer through the head end of each shrimp and the second skewer through the tail area so that the shrimp lie flat on the grate. Thread 6 shrimp on each set of double skewers.

On the remaining 2 skewers, thread the lemon and orange wedges, separately, lengthwise.

Place all the skewers in a flat non-metallic dish. Pour the lemon-orange mixture over the kabobs.

Refrigerate and marinate for 2–4 hours. Turn the kabobs over in the marinade after 1 hour.

Preheat the grill on medium-high (450–550°F/230–290°C) for 10 minutes with the lid closed. Using a pair of long-handled tongs, oil the grate by wiping it with a piece of folded paper towel dipped lightly in canola oil.

Place the kabobs on the grate and cook, lid open, for 3–4 minutes per side or until the shrimp have changed color and are just cooked through and the orange and lemon wedges are lightly charred. Do not overcook the shrimp.

Transfer shrimp kabobs to a serving plate and squeeze the orange and lemon wedges over the shrimp.

SESAME-CRUSTED SCALLOPS

24 large scallops

½ tsp (2 mL) garlic salt

¼ cup (60 mL) white sesame seeds

¼ cup (60 mL) melted butter

RINSE THE SCALLOPS and pat them dry with paper towel.

Remove the tough crescent-shaped muscle from the side of the scallops.

Put 6 scallops on each skewer, or use double skewers to prevent the scallops from rotating when the skewers are turned over on the grate. Leave a small space on the skewers between the scallops for more consistent cooking.

Mix the butter with the garlic salt. Place the skewered scallops on a large, flat plate and brush the garlic butter generously over the scallops.

Refrigerate the scallops for 30 minutes to solidify the butter.

Preheat the grill on high (550–600°F/290–315°C) for 10 minutes with the lid closed.

Using a pair of long-handled tongs, oil the grate by wiping it with a piece of folded paper towel dipped lightly in canola oil.

Reduce the heat to medium-high (450–550°F/230–290°C).

Place the sesame seeds on a large, flat plate or cutting board. Remove the scallops from the refrigerator. Roll the skewered scallops in the sesame seeds.

Grill the scallops for about 2–3 minutes per side with the lid closed.

The scallops are cooked when they turn white and feel slightly firm to touch. Do not overcook or they will become tough.

EASY CHEESY ORANGE ROUGHY

1½-lb (700 g) orange roughy

2 Tbsp (30 mL) extra-virgin olive oil, divided

⅛ tsp (0.5 mL) salt

⅛ tsp (0.5 mL) pepper

½ lemon, pulp and peel, finely diced

3 Tbsp (45 mL) capers

½ cup (125 mL) shredded cheddar cheese

CUT A PIECE of heavy-duty aluminum foil large enough to wrap loosely around the orange roughy. Brush 1 Tbsp (15 mL) olive oil on the aluminum foil.

Place the fish in the middle of the aluminum foil. Do not stack the fish.

Drizzle the remaining 1 Tbsp (15 mL) olive oil over the orange roughy. Sprinkle the salt, pepper, lemon, capers, and cheese over the fish.

Fold and securely seal the foil over the fish.

Preheat the grill on medium (350–450°F/175–230°C) for 10 minutes with the lid closed. Turn the heat to medium-low (300–350°F/150–175°C). Place the foil packet on the grate, sealed side up.

Cook with the lid closed for about 15 minutes. Do not overcook.

Santa Cruz, a Channel Islands Adventure

WE BOARDED AN Island Packers boat for the 20-mile (32 kilometer) crossing from Ventura Harbor to Santa Cruz, the largest of the Channel Islands off the southern coast of California. On an adventure for the day, we carried a prepared lunch, rain gear, and cameras. Other passengers transported kayaks, camping gear, and backpacks. Sea lions sunbathing on a buoy ignored us all.

The Santa Cruz terrain resembles a miniature California—the way it was before human discovery—with two mountain ranges, a central valley, deep canyons, and year-round springs and streams circled by miles of craggy coastline cliffs, sea caves, tide pools, and beaches.

A pair of ravens met us on the dock. The resident park ranger warned that ravens are capable of unzipping backpacks. Santa Cruz is also home to the island scrub jay and island fox—neither is found anywhere else in the world. As we spread our lunch out on a picnic table, two foxes, a little larger than domestic cats, walked around our feet and under the picnic table like puppies expecting scraps. Their fur was sandy red, their tails fluffy. We were tempted to feed them but we did not; we would be endangering them by doing so.

There is a web of trails on Santa Cruz Island. The Cavern Point trail follows rocky terrain through wildflowers to a panorama of the Santa Barbara Channel. We breathed in the scent of wild grasses warmed by sunshine and felt the heat radiating from the rocks. White-tailed birds sang overhead as we stood on a bluff to view waves crashing on a beach far below.

As we climbed back onto the Island Packers boat, a passenger reported a raven snatching her lip gloss. Our shoulder bags were noticeably lighter but solely because we were no longer carrying lunches. Nothing else was missing.

MOST POPULAR MARINATED SHRIMP

5 Tbsp (75 mL) extra-virgin olive oil

2 tsp (10 mL) Dijon mustard

4 tsp (20 mL) chopped garlic

4 tsp (20 mL) fresh lemon juice

5 Tbsp (75 mL) fresh orange juice

¾ tsp (4 mL) dried basil leaves

4 tsp (20 mL) white wine

16 jumbo shrimp

IN A BOWL, combine all ingredients but the shrimp. Stir well to thoroughly combine the flavors.

Add the shrimp to the marinade. Stir gently to thoroughly coat the shrimp. Cover and refrigerate for 1 hour.

Place a porcelain grill topper on the barbecue grate. Preheat the barbecue on medium-high (450–550°F/230–290°C) for 10 minutes with the lid closed. Using a pair of long-handed tongs, oil the grill topper by wiping it with a piece of folded paper towel dipped lightly in canola oil.

Place the shrimp side by side on the grill topper. Cook for 2–3 minutes per side, or until the shrimp become firm and pink. Do not overcook.

Over-the-Top Attractions

SELKIRK, MANITOBA, is named for Thomas Douglas, the Fifth Earl of Selkirk, the Scottish founder of the Red River Settlement in the southern Red River Valley. The town has a reputation for giant channel catfish with an average size of 15–20 lb (6.75–9 kg). Chuck, the fiberglass channel catfish, landed in Selkirk in 1986 in dedication to good sport and good fishing. He measures in at 25 feet (7.5 meters).

We discovered in our travels that Manitoba has more than one interesting over-the-top attraction. The following is just a sampling: the world's largest painting on an easel in Altona; the world's largest cookie jar in Deloraine; famous red-sided garter snakes in Inwood; the World's Largest/Tallest Purple Martin Colony in Neepewa; a wild turkey roadside attraction in La Riviere; a giant mosquito in Karmarno, also known as the mosquito capital of the world; the world's largest fire hydrant in Elm Creek; a giant Rolls Royce in Steinbach (the "automobile city"); an oil derrick in Virden; the Whispering Giant at Winnipeg Beach; the world's largest Coke can in Portage La Prairie; a canvasback duck in Minnedosa; a mallard duck in Petersfield; a viking ship in Erickson and a viking in Gimli; the Snow Goose in Dunrea; the world's largest smoking pipe in St. Claude; Sara the Camel in Glenboro; Tommy the Turtle in Boissevain; the world's largest sturgeon in Dominion City; an antique tractor in Austin; elk in Onanole; a windmill in Holland; Happy Rock in Gladstone; a spinning wheel in Sifton; a monument for Josiah Flintabbatey Flonatin in Flin Flon.

Chuck the Channel Cat is not alone in his mission to entertain visitors in Manitoba.

PAPRIKA CATFISH

2 tsp (10 mL) garlic salt

2 Tbsp (30 mL) paprika

2 tsp (10 mL) lemon pepper

Two 10–12 oz (300–340 g)
catfish fillets

Canola oil (for brushing)

IN A SMALL bowl, combine the dry ingredients. Mix thoroughly.

Place the catfish fillets in a flat dish. Pat the paprika mixture over the surface of the fillets. Cover the fish and refrigerate for 15–30 minutes.

Preheat the grill on medium-high (450–550°F/230–290°C) for 10 minutes with the lid closed. Using a pair of long-handled tongs, oil the grate by wiping it with a piece of folded paper towel dipped lightly in canola oil.

Brush the fish fillets on both sides with canola oil.

Grill the catfish with the lid closed for 3–4 minutes. Gently turn the fillets over and grill for another 3–4 minutes. The thickness of the fillets will determine the grilling time. The catfish is ready if it flakes when tested with a fork.

Erieau by Chance

LIKE A LOT of people, we discovered Erieau, Ontario, by chance. This fishing village sits at the tip of a peninsula jutting between Lake Erie and Rondeau Bay. A single road loops in and out.

Erieau is one of those hidden gems rapidly becoming a popular spot with cottagers, boaters, RVers, bikers, fishermen, and sun worshippers. Even though some locals would like to keep Erieau the way it is, the yellow perch, fresh produce, restaurants, brewpub, and expanse of public beaches are leading to change.

The village lies in Canada's deep south, on the migratory paths of birds and butterflies. On the days that Lake Erie thinks it is the Atlantic, waves crash onto jetties. When the lake behaves like the Mediterranean, people search the beach looking for sea glass, stroll the tree-lined boulevard, and head out for a day on the water.

On a daily basis, unique Great Lakes fishing boats that look more like shoeboxes than boats cast their nets offshore and haul in the prized yellow perch.

Whether a person catches their own or buys perch at a fish market, the ultimate seafood experience is the shore lunch—fish fresh from the hook into the frying pan.

PERCH SHORE LUNCH

½ cup (125 mL) flour

½ tsp (2 mL) salt

¼ tsp (1 mL) pepper

¼ cup (60 mL) beer, any style

1 egg

12 oz (340 g) large bag salt and vinegar potato chips

1 lb (450 g) perch fillets

2–4 Tbsp (30–60 mL) butter

3–4 cups (750–1000 mL) frozen hash browns

One 14-oz (398 mL) can baked beans in tomato sauce

IN A BOWL, combine the flour, salt, and pepper. Set aside.

Place the beer and the egg in a separate bowl. Whisk until well mixed. Set aside.

Put the potato chips in a resealable plastic bag. Crush the chips into small pieces. Place the crushed chips in a third bowl. Set aside.

Place an oiled griddle on the grill grate. Preheat the grill on high (550–600°F/290–315°C) for 10 minutes with the lid closed. Turn the heat down to medium (350–450°F/175–230°C).

Rinse the fillets. Pat the fish dry with paper towels. Dip the perch fillets into the bowl of flour. Shake excess flour away. Dip the fish into the egg mixture to coat the entire fillet with liquid. Dip the wet fillet into the crushed potato chips. Place the breaded fillets on a plate.

Melt the butter on the griddle. Place the hash browns on one side. Brown the potatoes.

Make a hole in the center of the hash browns on the griddle. Fill the hole with the baked beans.

Place the fillets in the butter on the open side of the griddle. Turn the fish after 5 minutes or when the breading is golden brown. Cook, lid down, for 2–3 minutes.

A Foodie's and a Photographer's Dream

PRINCE EDWARD ISLAND is the land of potato farms, fishing boats, Anne of Green Gables, lighthouses, and sunsets. Giant, round bales of hay dot fields of red soil stretching down to the shoreline. The unique red soil is the result of oxidization, the rusting of fine iron-compound particles in the island's sandstone. Under an enormous blue sky, row after row of flowering potato plants flow toward the ocean. Reflections of fishing boats and brightly painted fishing shacks shimmer in the water.

There are 20 lighthouses on Prince Edward Island, each with its individual day markings and flash patterns. First-generation lighthouses, those built before 1873, are an octagonal shape. They were constructed when timber was abundant. The second-generation lighthouse is square-tapered. Depletion of the timber supply by the shipbuilding industry forced the change.

One morning, we left the main roads and drove down a combination of red gravel and hard-packed clay to roads of red sand and fine red dust that were designated as unimproved. It was along one of these roads that we saw herds of cattle sporting red socks, their legs covered in red dust from hoof to knee.

On the north shore, in North Rustico, we sat on a sand dune, near a lighthouse, and watched the sun set over the harbor. Orange and red streaks spread across the sky as fishermen guided their boats silently into the narrow channel between sandbar and shore.

We spent a lazy afternoon indulging in the island's famous Malpeque oysters.

BACON-INFUSED MALPEQUE OYSTERS

24 Malpeque oysters

3 strips bacon, finely chopped, fried, and drained

3 Tbsp (45 mL) melted unsalted butter

2 tsp (10 mL) lemon juice

1 tsp (5 mL) garlic powder

¼ tsp (1 mL) cayenne pepper

1 tsp (5 mL) chopped fresh parsley

1 tsp (5 mL) chopped fresh cilantro

1 Tbsp (15 mL) finely grated Parmesan cheese

4 tsp (20 mL) breadcrumbs

DISCARD ANY OYSTERS that are not tightly clamped shut, or do not clamp shut when tapped. Store oysters, bowl-side down, in an open container covered with a wet paper towel or wet cloth in the refrigerator at 40°F (4°C). Do not store directly on ice, in water, or in a sealed plastic bag.

In a bowl, combine the bacon, butter, lemon juice, garlic powder, cayenne, parsley, and cilantro. Set aside.

In a small bowl, combine the Parmesan cheese and bread crumbs. Set aside.

With a brush, scrub the oyster shells under cold running water.

Preheat the grill on high (550–600°F/290–315°C) for 10 minutes with the lid closed.

Place the oysters, bowl-side down, on the hot grill grate. If the oysters are small, place them on a piece of foil.

Cook the oysters for 1 minute with the lid closed. The oysters should now be slightly open. Wearing a heavy oven mitt, quickly remove the oysters from the grill. Do not turn off the grill.

Use a shucking knife or a clean, flat screwdriver to pry open the oysters, taking care not to spill their nectar.

Slide a small, sharp knife between the oyster and the shell to sever the muscles, leaving the oyster in the bowl-shaped half shell.

Spoon ½ tsp (2 mL) of the bacon mixture on top of each oyster. Sprinkle with the cheese mixture.

Place the oysters on the hot grill. Close the lid.

Cook for about 5 minutes or until the butter bubbles and the edges of the oysters begin to curl slightly.

LAMB & GAME

Hawaii, Farm-to-Table Paradise

WHEN WE WERE in Hawaii, we met food producers who are working to combine the traditional food production methods and values of the past with modern technology. They are developing a farm-to-table system that embraces local food and sustainable farming practices.

At Hamakua Springs Country Farms, innovative methods are utilized on ancient land to grow crops and focus on solutions to the rising costs of energy. A young farmer raises Dorper hair sheep that are very suitable to the Hawaiian climate. Rather than produce wool, he raises the lambs for meat, which he sells at a farmers market. Taro, a traditional Hawaiian staple, is being grown with modern methods by a young farmer working his father's land. At Hamakua Heritage Farm, otherwise known as Hawaii's Gourmet Fungal Jungle, mushrooms are grown in jars by owners who moved to the Big Island after undergoing career changes. Two mainlanders established the Original Hawaiian Chocolate Factory. An east coast entrepreneur developed Kekela Farms to grow 30 different organic vegetables. Hawaii Beef Producers are working with other ranchers and restaurateurs to create awareness for Hawaiian grass-fed beef. The Holua-koa Café provides the ultimate farm to table experience with local fish, beef, veggies, and fruit. At his restaurant, Sam Choy's Kai Lanai, Sam Choy proudly prepares meals using entirely locally sourced ingredients. The Big Island Abalone Corporation pumps pure, cold, nutrient-rich seawater from the Pacific Ocean to create an environment for farming Kona Abalone.

By choice, and by necessity, Hawaiian lineal descendants, Hawaiian-born Hawaiians, and new arrivals to the islands are working together to bring the Hawaii they love back to the islands' roots of self-sufficiency and sustainability.

SMOKED ROLLED LEG OF LAMB WITH HERBS & SUN-DRIED TOMATOES

¼ cup (60 mL) fresh lemon juice

½ Tbsp (7.5 mL) finely chopped fresh thyme

½ Tbsp (7.5 mL) finely chopped fresh rosemary

½ Tbsp (7.5 mL) finely chopped fresh mint

¼ cup (60 mL) finely chopped fresh parsley

2 Tbsp (30 mL) extra-virgin olive oil

¾ cup (185 mL) sun-dried tomatoes, chopped into small pieces

½ cup (125 mL) red wine vinegar

½ cup (125 mL) canola oil

1 tsp (5 mL) finely chopped garlic

½ tsp (2 mL) sea salt

½ tsp (2 mL) coarsely ground pepper

2 long sprigs fresh rosemary

2 long sprigs fresh thyme

4–6 lb (1.8–2.7 kg) boneless leg of lamb

IN A BOWL, combine the lemon juice, thyme, rosemary, mint, parsley, and olive oil. Stir in the sun-dried tomato pieces. Cover and set aside for 1 hour to allow the flavors to blend together.

In a separate bowl, make the basting sauce by combining the vinegar, canola oil, garlic, salt, and pepper. Set aside.

Make a basting brush by tying the sprigs of rosemary and thyme together with kitchen twine.

Place the lamb on a cutting board. Trim away fat and sinew. Butterfly any thick areas of the meat to make it lie as flat as possible. At this stage the lamb may not be one perfect piece. For ease of rolling, the meat could be divided into 2 roasts.

Cut 4 lengths of kitchen twine, about 18 inches (46 cm) each. Place the twine at even intervals under the meat with equal lengths extending out both sides. Cut 2 lengths of kitchen twine about 24 inches (60 cm) long. Place the twine lengthwise under the meat.

Spread the sun-dried tomato mixture evenly over the meat. Roll the meat like a cigar. Tuck any loose pieces into the center. Tie the twine tightly to secure the roll. Trim away excess twine.

Preheat the smoker to medium (275°F/140°C). Brush the lamb with basting sauce. Place the lamb on the grate.

Cook with the lid closed for about 2¼ hours or until the internal temperature registers 135°F (57°C) on an instant-read thermometer for medium-rare, or to desired doneness.

Using the herb brush, baste with the basting sauce every 30 minutes.

Remove the lamb from the smoker, tent with foil. Rest for 15 minutes before carving.

Remove the twine and carve the lamb.

LAMB LOIN CHOPS WITH ORANGE ZEST

Eight 4–5 oz (110–140 g) lamb
loin chops

1 tsp (5 mL) garlic powder

1 tsp (5 mL) sea salt

1 tsp (5 mL) coarsely ground pepper

2 tsp (10 mL) extra-virgin olive oil

1 Tbsp (15 mL) brown sugar

1 Tbsp (15 mL) orange juice

1 Tbsp (15 mL) finely chopped
orange zest

TRIM ANY EXCESS fat from the edges of the lamb chops.

In a bowl, combine the garlic powder, salt, pepper, and oil.

Rub the paste on both sides of the lamb chops. Cover or wrap the chops in plastic wrap and refrigerate for 2 hours.

Preheat the grill on medium-high (450–550°F/230–290°C) for 10 minutes with the lid closed. Using a pair of long-handled tongs, oil the grate by wiping it with a piece of folded paper towel dipped lightly in canola oil.

In a bowl, combine brown sugar and orange juice.

Remove the chops from the refrigerator. Spoon the orange juice mixture on one side of the chops. Place the chops on the hot grate, orange juice–side down.

Close the lid and grill for 4 minutes.

Spoon the orange juice mixture on each chop. Turn the chops over.

Close the lid and grill for 3 minutes or until an instant-read thermometer registers 135°F (57°C) for medium-rare, or to desired doneness.

Remove from grill. Sprinkle orange zest over the chops before serving.

SMOKED VENISON ROAST

⅓ cup + 1 tsp (85 mL) peanut oil

2 lb (900 g) venison roast

1 Tbsp (15 mL) pepper

1 tsp (5 mL) dried thyme leaves

1 tsp (5 mL) dried sage leaves

1 tsp (5 mL) dry mustard

6 garlic cloves, chopped

1½ cups (375 mL) ginger ale

3 bay leaves

½ cup (125 mL) chopped onion

SIPHON THE PEANUT oil into an injector needle (kitchen syringe). Inject the venison with the oil in several places, inserting only a little bit of oil at a time.

In a small bowl, combine the pepper, thyme, sage, and dry mustard. Rub it over the entire surface of the roast.

In a large bowl, mix the remaining ingredients. Place the venison in the liquid and cover tightly with plastic wrap. Refrigerate for 24 hours, turning the roast once or twice to marinate all sides.

Remove the roast from the marinade. Discard the marinade.

Preheat the smoker to medium-high (300°F/150°C) using mesquite wood.

Cook the venison for approximately 2 hours or until the internal temperature registers 150–160°F (66–71°C) on an instant-read thermometer for medium doneness.

Remove the venison from the smoker and tent loosely with aluminum foil for 15 minutes. Slice against the grain.

The Winter People

IT WAS MID-AUGUST when we flew into Tuktoyaktuk, Northwest Territories, on the shore of the Beaufort Sea. There was no snow. There were no bugs. Sled dogs and snowmobiles sat idle, waiting. The residents of Tuktoyaktuk are winter people.

Transportation to Tuktoyaktuk in the winter does not require getting on an airplane. Frozen ice roads are formed across the tundra, lakes, and rivers. Northerners travel these ice roads by car, truck, dog team, and snowmobile to connect with friends and family, conduct business, and get supplies.

We learned about their underground icehouses that utilize the deep frozen soil. Typically, a ladder goes down approximately 30 feet (9 meters) to access the underground system of alleyways and compartments. A pulley system of pails and drums is used to lower caribou, whale meat, and geese—the staples of the northern diet.

The people of the North respect permafrost, the thick subsurface layer of soil that remains frozen throughout the year. They build their houses on pilings in order to leave the permafrost undisturbed, thus guaranteeing a solid footing.

In the fall and winter, families go out on the frozen tundra to hunt and fish for their annual food supply. Two beluga whales—with their layer of blubber that renders itself down at room temperature to be used as a dip for meat and a preservative for fish—along with 60–80 geese and 20–25 caribou, will sustain a family of five for a year.

CARIBOU STEAKS

¾ cup (185 mL) red wine

1½ Tbsp (23 mL) canola oil + extra (for brushing)

Pinch of ground ginger

¼ tsp (1 mL) hot sauce

1 whole clove

1 garlic clove, chopped

1 Tbsp (15 mL) dried cranberries

Four 6–8 oz (170–230 g) caribou steaks (½ inch/1 cm thick)

IN A BOWL, combine all ingredients but the caribou. Mix well.

Place the marinade in a resealable plastic bag. Add the steaks. Seal tightly and place on a flat plate in the refrigerator for 48 hours. Turn the bag over at least once while the steaks marinate.

Remove the steaks and discard the marinade.

Preheat the grill on high (550–600°F/290–315°C) for 10 minutes with the lid closed.

Using a pair of long-handled tongs, oil the grate by wiping it with a piece of folded paper towel dipped lightly in canola oil. Lower the heat to medium-high (450–550°F/230–290°C).

Brush the steaks with canola oil. Place the steaks on the grate immediately after oiling them.

Grill the steaks about 2 minutes on each side with the lid closed. Do not overcook this lean meat.

Crossing the Arctic Circle

THE DEMPSTER HIGHWAY in Canada runs north from the Yukon to the Northwest Territories. It is the only public highway in North America to cross the Arctic Circle. It crosses the Mackenzie River Delta and stretches between mountains that have never seen a glacier. It crosses terrain where the great porcupine caribou spend the winter.

The Dempster travels through Beringia, an ancient place believed to be the point of entry for the human species into the New World. This bridge between North America and Asia was the last continental land mass to be colonized by humans from 40,000–10,000 years ago, when predators of staggering proportions competed with human hunters for food, and plants and animals struggled to survive the cold, dry, treeless terrain.

We stood in peace and awe on the land where ancient peoples lived and traveled. Miles and miles of northern tundra spread out before us. We experienced complete and unblemished silence.

The caribou have lived in both North America and Asia for nearly two million years. The myths and legends of many of today's First Nations are rich in information about the animals. The caribou was and is still crucial to human survival. Northern diets include it roasted, fried, baked, dried, and raw. A sign along the Dempster Highway asks hunters to hunt safely, to aim for organs vital for the kill, and only to hunt the caribou to fill a need.

The roast we prepared in this recipe came from the remote Rankin Inlet in Nunavut.

ROTISSERIE CARIBOU ROAST

2 cups (500 mL) red wine

3 Tbsp (45 mL) canola oil

⅛ tsp (0.5 mL) ground ginger

½ tsp (2 mL) hot sauce

2 whole cloves

2 garlic cloves, chopped

2 Tbsp (30 mL) dried cranberries

2 lb (900 g) inside round caribou roast

1 lb (450 g) sliced bacon

2 cups (500 mL) water

2 fresh sprigs of rosemary

IN A BOWL, combine the wine, oil, ginger, hot sauce, cloves, garlic, and cranberries. Mix well.

Place the marinade in a large resealable plastic bag. Add the caribou roast. Seal the bag tightly and place the bag flat on a plate in the refrigerator. Marinate for 48 hours. Turn the bag over at least once while the caribou marinates.

Remove the roast from the marinade. Save the marinade.

Cover the entire roast with strips of bacon. Use kitchen string to hold the bacon in place by wrapping the string lengthwise and crosswise around the roast.

Insert the rotisserie rod through the roast lengthwise. Attach the rod to the rotisserie.

Place a drip pan under the roast. Pour the saved marinade and the water into the drip pan. Add the rosemary sprigs. Add more water to the drip pan if necessary.

Light the rotisserie flame on high (550–600°F/290–315°C) then adjust the heat to medium (350–450°F/175–230°C). With the lid closed, cook the roast for about 90 minutes or until the internal temperature of the roast registers 135°F (57°C) on an instant-read thermometer for medium-rare. Caribou is a very lean meat; overcooking will toughen it and dry it out.

Remove the roast from the rotisserie. Tent loosely with foil. Rest for 15 minutes before carving.

VEGETABLES

Paradise for Gardeners and Birdwatchers

SOUTHWESTERN ONTARIO IS a prosperous agricultural area with a climate among the mildest in Canada. Blanketed between the spring and autumn bird migrations, the hot, humid summers yield a wide variety of vegetable crops. It is not unusual to see entire fields of tomatoes, peppers, carrots, broccoli, cauliflower, squash, and sweet potatoes. Southwestern Ontario also produces sweet, sweet onions, like the ones we use to create our Sweet Onion & Cheese Pie (see next page).

Point Pelee National Park in southwestern Ontario marks the southernmost point of the Canadian mainland, at the 42nd parallel. By sharing latitude with Rome, Barcelona, and northern California, the long, slender oasis that cozies up to the north shore of Lake Erie has more rare plants and animals than any other region in Canada.

Bird migration was the reason Point Pelee became a national park. Comprised of marsh, forest, fields, and beaches, the park provides first-class birding opportunities in the spring and fall. It is also a gathering place for monarch butterflies as they plan their annual autumn trip to Mexico.

We spent a day in Pelee National Park as novice birders. The air was alive with the "sweet-sweet, sweet-sweet" of the yellow warbler and the hungry kitten cry of the gray catbird.

We discovered bird-watchers are a special species of people. They speak quietly and sparingly. Bird chirping holds priority over human conversation. Whenever we came across a cluster of binoculars pointed in the same direction, we knew we were about to enjoy a rare find like the eastern screech owl or the scarlet tanager.

SWEET ONION & CHEESE PIE

4 tsp (20 mL) white balsamic vinegar

1 Tbsp (15 mL) brown sugar

1 tsp (5 mL) salt

½ tsp (2 mL) pepper

½ tsp (2 mL) ground nutmeg

½ cup (125 mL) shredded mozzarella

½ cup (125 mL) shredded cheddar cheese

4 medium-sized mild onions, peeled

1 Tbsp (15 mL) butter

1 Tbsp (15 mL) extra-virgin olive oil + extra (for brushing)

1 uncooked piecrust (found in the refrigerated section of grocery stores, or homemade)

IN A BOWL, combine the vinegar, brown sugar, salt, pepper, and nutmeg. Mix well. Set aside.

In a separate bowl, combine shredded cheeses. Mix well. Set aside.

Cut the onions in half lengthwise. Remove any tough cores. Cut each half into thin slices lengthwise. Set aside.

Stir the butter and olive oil in a frying pan over medium-high heat until the butter is melted.

Add the onion slices. Cook and stir the onions for about 5 minutes or until they are translucent and soft.

Reduce the heat to medium and stir in the balsamic vinegar mixture.

Cook and stir for 10–12 minutes or until the onions are browned and caramelized. Remove the onions from the heat to cool.

Cover a cookie sheet with parchment paper. Place the piecrust flat on the parchment paper.

Place ¾ cup (185 mL) of the cheese mixture in the center of the piecrust.

Pile the onions high on top of the cheese. Leave about 1 inch (2.5 cm) of the crust uncovered around the outside rim. Sprinkle the remaining ¼ cup (60 mL) of cheese over the onions.

Fold the edges of the dough up over the onions, creasing the pastry as needed, to enclose the onions except for a small circle in the top center of the pie.

Preheat the grill on high (550–600°F/290–315°C) for 10 minutes with the lid closed.

Prepare the grill for indirect cooking. Turn one side of the grill off and leave the other side on medium-high (450–550°F/230–290°C) heat to maintain a temperature of about 375–400°F (190–200°C).

Brush the outside of the pastry lightly with olive oil.

Place the cookie sheet on the unlit side of the grate. Bake over indirect heat for about 30 minutes or until the crust is cooked through and golden brown. Rotate the pie halfway through baking time, if necessary, to prevent burning on one side.

Remove the pie from the grill and let stand for 10 minutes before serving.

We Could Live in These Shops

LITTLE ITALY IN Boston's North End is a place where flowers hang from balconies of five-storey, red brick, walk-up condominiums. There is no such thing as a supermarket or big-box store in this neighborhood.

Down an alley, we step into Bricco Panetteria, a one-room, white-tiled, flour-dusted bakery where artisan bread made only with natural ingredients is produced in tight quarters.

We are warned before we enter Maria's Pastry Shop that the owner is not overly hospitable. A sign on the bakery wall says "You call it chaos we call it family" and another, closer to the ovens, says "Do you want to talk to the man in charge or to the woman who knows what is going on." Maria has owned the shop for 32 years. Her cannoli is heavenly.

Polcari's Coffee on the corner of Salem and Parmenter is the place to go for roasted coffee beans, wild oregano, pomegranate molasses, grey salt, and preserved lemons.

Nearby Alba Produce is a small greengrocer. Produce is unpriced and off limits. No one but the vendor is allowed to touch the vegetables. If customers do not like what he picks, they are encouraged to point to the item they prefer.

The Bricco Salumeria & Pasta Shoppe is a deli bursting with cured meats, cheeses, tomatoes, olive oils, and vinegars. We sampled balsamic vinegars as smooth and sweet as wine from Italy, where men are known to carry a vial of it in their breast pockets.

With our Roasted & Marinated Red Peppers recipe (see next page), we revisit the flavors and aromas of Boston's Little Italy with our hand picked peppers, fine herbs, extra-virgin olive oil, and aged balsamic vinegar.

ROASTED & MARINATED RED PEPPERS

2 large red bell peppers

4 tsp (20 mL) balsamic vinegar

2 Tbsp (30 mL) extra-virgin olive oil +
2 tsp (10 mL) for brushing the peppers

1 Tbsp (15 mL) finely chopped
fresh basil

1 Tbsp (15 mL) finely chopped cilantro

1 garlic clove, finely chopped

½ tsp (2 mL) sea salt

¼ tsp (1 mL) pepper

CUT THE RED peppers in quarters, lengthwise. Remove the seeds, membranes, and stem.

Preheat the grill on high (550–600°F/290–315°C) for 10 minutes with the lid closed. Using a pair of long-handled tongs, oil the grate by wiping it with a piece of folded paper towel dipped lightly in canola oil.

Brush the pepper strips on all sides with 2 tsp (10 mL) olive oil.

Grill the red pepper, skin-side down, with the lid closed, about 10 minutes or until the skin is charred. Turn the peppers over and grill for about 3 minutes.

Transfer the peppers to a bowl and cover tightly with plastic wrap for 15 minutes.

Remove and discard blackened skin from the peppers. Save any juice.

In a small bowl, combine the vinegar, 2 Tbsp (30 mL) oil, herbs, garlic, salt, pepper, and pepper juice.

Place the peppers in a large bowl. Pour the balsamic mixture over the peppers. Toss and refrigerate for 1 hour before serving.

LEMON-HERBED SWEET & WHITE POTATOES

2 medium-sized white potatoes, unpeeled

2 medium-sized sweet potatoes, peeled

2 Tbsp (30 mL) extra-virgin olive oil + extra (for brushing)

3 Tbsp (45 mL) fresh lemon juice

2 tsp (10 mL) dried rosemary leaves, crumbled

¼ tsp (1 mL) pepper

¼ tsp (1 mL) salt

CUT THE WHITE potatoes and sweet potatoes into ¼-inch (6 mm) thick rounds.

In a bowl, combine the remaining ingredients.

Place 2 large pieces of heavy-duty aluminum foil side by side on the counter. Brush olive oil over the surface of the sheets of foil.

Alternating white and sweet potato slices, create a row of potato slices in the middle of each piece of foil.

Brush the oil and lemon mixture over the potatoes. Let the mixture trickle between and around the potato slices. Seal the sheets of foil around the potatoes leaving air pockets inside for steaming.

Preheat the grill on high (550–600°F/290–315°C) for 10 minutes with the lid closed. Turn the heat down to medium (350–450°F/175–230°C) and place the potato packages on the grate.

Cook the potatoes, with the lid closed, for about 20 minutes or until the potatoes are tender. Turn the packages over halfway through the grilling time.

Pan de Campo Cook-Off

THE PAN DE Campo Cook-Off takes place annually in an open field behind the American Legion in Edinburg, Texas. Pan de campo is cowboy flatbread cooked in a Dutch oven over an open fire. Competitors and judges dress in cowboy attire—cowboy boots, jeans, shirts, and hats. Traditionally, the flatbread was prepared at the end of a long day of driving cattle on both sides of the US-Mexican border.

Participants arrive early in the day to position their pick-up trucks and light their mesquite campfires. They set up their coolers, arrange cooking pots, and mix their dough ingredients—flour, baking powder, salt, sugar, oil, and milk. Some add a secret ingredient hoping it will give them the edge over their competitors. Deep cast iron pots are positioned in campfires. The dough is tossed until it is flat and round, and then placed inside the pot. Hot, glowing coals are spread over the lid. The pan de campo comes out golden brown, almost crunchy, and delicious with a cup of chuck wagon coffee.

The Ladies' Auxiliary at the Legion sells *menudo*. Served with corn tortillas for dipping, it is a traditional Mexican soup with greasy broth, beans, tripe, and chili peppers. Usually eaten after a night out on the town, it is widely proclaimed to be antidotal for a hangover because it is said to stimulate the senses, soothe the stomach, and clear the head.

Of the two traditional dishes, our northern palates preferred the cowboy flatbread to the menudo.

SEASONED POTATO WEDGES

1 Tbsp (15 mL) seasoned salt

1 Tbsp (15 mL) lemon pepper

¾ tsp (4 mL) garlic powder

¾ tsp (4 mL) onion powder

¾ tsp (4 mL) ground coriander

4 medium roasting potatoes, unpeeled

¼ cup (60 mL) extra-virgin olive oil

IN A LARGE bowl, combine the dry ingredients. Set aside.

Cut the potatoes in half lengthwise. Cut each half into 4 wedges.

In a large bowl, toss the potato wedges with the olive oil.

Remove the potato wedges from the oil and place them in the bowl of spices. Toss to coat the wedges evenly with the spices.

Preheat the grill on medium (350–450°F/175–230°C) for 10 minutes with the lid closed.

Place a flat porcelain grill topper on the grill grate. Using a pair of long-handled tongs, oil the grill topper by wiping it with a piece of folded paper towel dipped lightly in canola oil.

Place the potato wedges side by side flat on the grill topper. Cook the potato wedges with the lid closed for 5–7 minutes per side or until tender.

PARMESAN GRILLED ASPARAGUS

24 large asparagus spears

¼ cup (60 mL) extra-virgin olive oil

1 tsp (5 mL) garlic powder

1 tsp (5 mL) pepper

1 tsp (5 mL) salt

1 Tbsp (15 mL) lemon juice

At least 1 Tbsp (15 mL) grated Parmesan cheese

TRIM AND DISCARD any tough ends from the asparagus spears. Place the asparagus flat on a plate.

In a bowl, combine all remaining ingredients but the Parmesan cheese. Mix well.

Brush the olive oil mixture over the asparagus, coating each spear.

Preheat the grill on high (550–600°F/290–315°C) for 10 minutes with the lid closed. Using a pair of long-handled tongs, oil the grate by wiping it with a piece of folded paper towel dipped lightly in canola oil. Reduce the heat to medium (350–450°F/175–230°C).

Place the asparagus spears side by side across the grate. If the asparagus spears are small, place them on an oiled grill topper on the grate.

Cook for 2–4 minutes on each side with the lid open. Small asparagus spears will cook faster.

Place the asparagus on a serving plate and sprinkle with grated Parmesan cheese.

GRILLED EGGPLANT

¼ cup (60 mL) extra-virgin olive oil

2 Tbsp (30 mL) balsamic vinegar

½ tsp (2 mL) salt

¼ tsp (1 mL) pepper

1 large eggplant, sliced into ½-inch (1 cm) rounds

¼ cup (60 mL) grated Parmesan cheese

PREHEAT THE GRILL on high (550–600°F/290–315°C) for 10 minutes with the lid closed.

Using a pair of long-handled tongs, oil the grate by wiping it with a piece of folded paper towel dipped lightly in canola oil. Turn the grill down to medium (350–450°F/175–230°C).

In a bowl, combine the oil, vinegar, salt, and pepper.

Brush the eggplant slices generously with the olive oil mixture to coat both sides of each slice.

Grill the eggplant 4–5 minutes on each side with the lid closed. Brush the top sides with the olive oil mixture before and after turning.

Transfer the eggplant to a plate and sprinkle the grated Parmesan cheese over top.

GRILLED BABY BOK CHOY

3 baby bok choy

3 Tbsp (45 mL) extra-virgin olive oil

1½ Tbsp (23 mL) rice wine vinegar

1½ Tbsp (23 mL) white sugar

½ tsp (2 mL) garlic powder

½ tsp (2 mL) anise seeds

Sea salt, to taste

Coarsely ground pepper, to taste

RINSE THE BOK choy under running water. Slice each bok choy in half lengthwise to make 6 pieces, leaving the root ends intact to keep each half from falling apart. Rinse again to remove any leftover grit. Set the bok choy on paper towels to dry.

Preheat the grill on medium (350–450°F/175–230°C) for 10 minutes with the lid closed. Using a pair of long-handled tongs, oil the grate by wiping it with a piece of folded paper towel dipped lightly in canola oil.

In a small bowl, combine the oil, vinegar, sugar, garlic powder, and anise seeds. Stir until sugar is dissolved.

Place the bok choy in a large bowl. Brush generously on all sides with the olive oil mixture.

Place a narrow piece of aluminum foil on the grate. Position the leafy end of the bok choy, cut-side up, on the foil to prevent the leaves from charring too soon. Grill, lid closed, for 3 minutes.

Turn the bok choy over and remove the foil. Grill for an additional 2 minutes or until tender-crisp and lightly charred.

Transfer bok choy to a platter. Sprinkle with salt and pepper.

Bumping Along the Trent-Severn Waterway

ONE SUMMER WE switched our motor home for a houseboat, and we soon discovered that operating a house on water is nothing like driving a home on wheels. Our highway was the Trent-Severn Waterway in Ontario, a 240-mile (385 kilometer) system of locks and dams connecting lakes and rivers between Trenton, on the Bay of Quinte, and Port Severn. Our traffic lights were green and red buoys.

The actual construction of the formalized waterway began in 1833, in Bobcaygeon, and took 87 years. The popular tourist spot in east-central Ontario is now known as Lock 32. It seemed logical that we should start our voyage in Bobcaygeon.

There are 41 locks, a marine railway, and two hydraulic lift locks along the Trent-Severn Waterway. The lock in Bobcaygeon is one of 37 conventional locks that act like steps in a water staircase to transport a boat from one level of water to another. There are no pumps required. The entire operation is accomplished with valves and gravity.

With gentle guidance from the lockmaster, we bumped our way in and out of Lock 32 and every other lock for the next four days. The good news is our friends, also non-boaters, whom we talked into sharing the experience, are still our friends.

LOADED ZUCCHINI BOATS

8 cherry tomatoes, chopped

4 tsp (20 mL) chopped red onion

4 tsp (20 mL) shredded mozzarella cheese

2 tsp (10 mL) chopped fresh oregano

1 tsp (5 mL) garlic powder

½ Tbsp (7.5 mL) white balsamic vinegar

4 tsp (20 mL) extra-virgin olive oil + extra (for brushing)

¼ tsp (1 mL) salt

¼ tsp (1 mL) pepper

4 small green zucchini

4 tsp (20 mL) shredded Parmesan cheese

IN A BOWL, combine all ingredients but the zucchini and Parmesan. Set aside.

Cut the zucchini in half lengthwise. Do not trim the ends. Cut a thin slice off the bottom of each half in order to create a flat surface so the zucchini boats don't roll over.

Scoop out the center pulp of the zucchini halves, leaving ¼ inch (6 mm) of pulp and skin.

Brush the cut side of the zucchini with olive oil.

Preheat the grill on medium (350–450°F/175–230°C) for 10 minutes with the lid closed. Using a pair of long-handled tongs, oil the grate by wiping it with a piece of folded paper towel dipped lightly in canola oil.

Grill the zucchini, cut-side down, for 3 minutes to create grill marks. Do not thoroughly cook the flesh. Transfer the zucchini to a platter, cavity side up. Do not turn the grill off.

Turn one side of the grill off and leave the other side on medium heat to maintain a temperature of 300–350°F (150–175°C).

Fill the zucchini cavities with the tomato mixture. Top the mixture with Parmesan cheese.

Place the zucchini boats on the unlit side of the grill. Grill for 7–10 minutes or until the cheese is melted, the tomatoes are hot, and the zucchini is cooked to tender-crisp.

STEAMED CORN ON THE COB

4 cobs of corn

1½ cups (375 mL) water

REMOVE THE HUSKS and silk from the corncobs. Trim the ends. Cut each cob in half.

Place 2 pieces of heavy-duty aluminum foil on the counter. Fold up the sides to form the foil into 2 large packets.

Place 4 corn halves, side by side, in each foil packet. Do not pile.

Add ¾ cup (185 mL) water to each packet. Seal the packets securely, leaving room for the corn to steam.

Preheat the grill on high (550–600°F/290–315°C) for 10 minutes with the lid closed.

Place the corn packets on the grate. Cook with the lid closed until the water in the packets begins to boil, about 8 minutes.

Transfer the packets from the grate to the raised grill shelf. Continue to cook on the shelf for 10–15 minutes with the lid closed.

BALSAMIC TARRAGON ROOT VEGETABLES

¼ cup (60 mL) white balsamic vinegar

2 Tbsp (30 mL) extra-virgin olive oil

1 tsp (5 mL) finely chopped fresh tarragon

1 clove garlic, peeled and chopped

1 cup (250 mL) peeled parsnip, cut into 1-inch (2.5 cm) rounds

1 cup (250 mL) peeled carrot, cut into 1-inch (2.5 cm) rounds

1 cup (250 mL) peeled turnip, cut into 1-inch (2.5 cm) cubes

1 cup (250 mL) peeled potato, cut into 1-inch (2.5 cm) cubes

IN A BOWL, combine the balsamic vinegar, olive oil, tarragon, and garlic.

Add the root vegetables to the bowl. Toss to coat them with the balsamic mixture.

Place a large, double layer of heavy-duty aluminum foil on the counter.

Place the vegetables in the center of the foil. Pour the balsamic mixture over the vegetables.

Seal the package tightly.

Preheat the grill on high (550–600°F/290–315°C) for 10 minutes with the lid closed. Turn the heat down to medium (350–450°F/175–230°C).

Grill the vegetables for 15–20 minutes with the lid closed. Turn the package over every 5 minutes during the cooking time.

The Long Climb to Julian

WE WERE TAKING our chances when we chose to drive the indirect route from El Centro to San Diego by turning north to wind through the Cuyamaca Mountains to Julian, California, 4,226 feet (1,288 meters) above sea level. The road would not be a problem in the summer, but we tackled it in December. We ascended and descended and maneuvered double s-curves. Luckily, there was no snow.

Julian, a historic gold mining town, is known for its apples, apple pies, and apple cider. In October, people arrive for the fall colors and the Apple Days Festival, when 10,000 apple pies are baked every week.

Just a bend and a hill out of town, we stopped at Jeremy's on the Hill, a California-style bistro. Jeremy Manley has lived in Julian all his life. Neighboring ranchers, vintners, vegetable growers, and fruit producers drop their goods off at his kitchen door and he transforms them into tantalizing dishes. A Cordon Bleu-trained chef who has been cooking since he was 10, Jeremy's philosophy is to keep food fresh, simple, and tasting great.

His garlic herb fries with chipotle aioli, grass-fed burgers, quinoa bowls, and handcrafted, pretty-as-a-picture desserts bring people up the mountain regularly.

Jeremy's brussels sprouts are tart, smokey, and naturally sweet like vegetable candy.

We planned an apple recipe to accompany this story, but Jeremy's brussels sprouts won us over. Our recipe (see next page), featuring sweet pickles and bacon, adds another dimension to the vegetable.

BACON BRUSSELS SPROUTS

20 brussels sprouts, trimmed, cut in half through the core

2 tsp (10 mL) extra-virgin olive oil

¼ tsp (1 mL) pepper

4 strips bacon, finely chopped

2 Tbsp (30 mL) finely chopped sweet pickles

OIL A SOLID barbecue wok and place on the grate.

Preheat the grill on high (550–600°F/290–315°C) for 10 minutes with the lid closed.

In a bowl, toss the brussels sprouts with the oil and pepper. Add the bacon and toss again.

Place the brussels sprouts mixture in the wok. Cook with the lid closed for 15–20 minutes or until the bacon is cooked and the sprouts are lightly charred. Stir every 2 minutes.

Transfer to a bowl and stir in the sweet pickles.

PORTOBELLO MUSHROOM STEAKS

3 Tbsp (45 mL) extra-virgin olive oil

4 tsp (20 mL) Worcestershire sauce

1 tsp (5 mL) soy sauce

¼ tsp (1 mL) pepper

½ tsp (2 mL) garlic powder

4 tsp (20 mL) balsamic vinegar

¼ tsp (1 mL) white sugar

2 tsp (10 mL) steak sauce

4 large Portobello mushrooms

IN A SMALL bowl, combine all ingredients but the mushrooms. Whisk together.

Rinse the mushroom caps. Pat dry. Trim stems to below the lip of the cap. Place mushrooms in a flat dish, cavity side down. Spoon the marinade over the caps. Cover. Refrigerate for 15 minutes.

Turn the mushrooms over, spoon marinade into the cavities and marinate for 15 minutes longer.

Preheat the grill on medium (350–450°F/175–230°C) for 10 minutes with the lid closed. Using a pair of long-handled tongs, oil the grate by wiping it with a piece of folded paper towel dipped lightly in canola oil.

Grill the mushrooms, cavity side up, for 4 minutes, lid closed. Turn the mushrooms over and grill, cavity side down, for 4 minutes, lid closed.

THYME-TOSSED VEGETABLES

¼ cup (60 mL) extra-virgin olive oil

1 Tbsp (15 mL) chopped fresh thyme

¼ tsp (1 mL) salt

¼ tsp (1 mL) pepper

1 small green zucchini,
cut into ¾-inch (2 cm) rounds

½ red bell pepper, seeded, cut into
2-inch (5 cm) pieces

½ green bell pepper, seeded,
cut into 2-inch (5 cm) pieces

½ red onion, cut into large wedges

6 brown mushrooms

2 medium beets, peeled,
cut into ½-inch (1 cm) slices

IN A LARGE bowl, combine the oil, thyme, salt, and pepper. Mix well.

Add the vegetables to the olive oil mixture. Toss well. Separate the beets from the other vegetables.

Preheat the grill on medium (350–450°F/175–230°C) for 10 minutes with the lid closed. Place an oiled square grill wok on the grate.

Place the beets in the wok and grill for 1–2 minutes on each side. Add the remaining vegetables and cook for 10–12 minutes. Turn the vegetables every 3 minutes, moving faster-cooking vegetables to the top of the vegetable mixture. Remove from the grill and serve.

Barge Power

TO ESCAPE RUSH-HOUR traffic in Washington, DC, we took a taxi to Georgetown where everyone goes for the restaurants, shopping, and nightlife.

A late-afternoon stroll took us behind the bistros and boutiques to a little-known spot of history along the C&O (Chesapeake and Ohio) Canal. From 1850 until 1924, a fleet of independently owned mule-drawn barges transported coal along the canal to bypass the thundering waterfalls on the Potomac River.

Entire families, known as canalers, lived aboard the barges. One member of the family was always on duty to yell "low bridge" as they floated under an overhead crossing. The women on the barges were among the first to use safety pins to attach their aprons to their dresses.

A unique diet went along with the canalers' lifestyle. Picnic ham, eel pie, boatman bean soup, turtle, and groundhog were standard fare. The children picked berries as they walked along the path with the mules. The first two rows of corn in the fields along the canal were designated for the boatmen and their families.

We met Molly and Nell, the mules that walked along a well-worn path, pulling the replica barge through the 15-foot (4.5 meters) wide canal. The barge was 13½ feet (4 meters) wide, leaving only inches to spare on each side.

GRILLED LIME & CILANTRO SWEET CORN

4 large cobs of corn, husks and silk removed

2 Tbsp (30 mL) butter, melted

2 Tbsp (30 mL) fresh lime juice

1 Tbsp (15 mL) finely chopped fresh cilantro

¼ tsp (1 mL) smoked paprika

Pinch of salt

PREHEAT THE GRILL on medium-high (450–550°F/230–290°C) for 10 minutes with the lid closed. Using a pair of long-handled tongs, oil the grate by wiping it with a piece of folded paper towel dipped lightly in canola oil.

In a bowl, combine the butter, lime juice, cilantro, paprika, and salt.

Generously brush each cob of corn with the lime-butter mixture and place on the grate.

Cook for about 20 minutes, turning every 3–5 minutes, with the lid open, until all sides are slightly charred.

Remove the corn from the grill and brush with any remaining lime-butter mixture. Serve immediately.

Vancouver's Chinatown

VANCOUVER, BRITISH COLUMBIA, has the second-largest Chinatown district in North America after San Francisco. Even the telephone booths have pagoda-style roofs. Street signs, business signs, and national banks are lettered in both English and Chinese.

Chinatown is a colorful collage of reds, greens, and golds. Shops sell bamboo, jade, brass, and silk. Open-air markets display dried fish, dried mushrooms, spices, and fresh produce. Many of these markets double as alternative pharmacies with doctors on hand to prescribe traditional Chinese remedies.

The streets are an eclectic combination of restaurants, bars, temples, and tea shops. Restaurants are known for their authentic *dim sum,* a succession of small tasty dishes often served on steaming hot bamboo trays. Outside one restaurant, a guitar hangs above the sidewalk as a shrine to Jimmy Hendrix. As a young boy he lived in Chinatown with his grandmother.

A quiet spot in the midst of all the commercial activity and heritage buildings is the Dr. Sun Yat-Sen Classical Chinese Garden that opened during Expo in 1986. Named after the founding father of the Republic of China, the full-scale classical Chinese garden is modeled upon private gardens from the Ming Dynasty. It is an oasis in the inner city, memorable for its delicate balance of natural vegetation, rocks and pools, fish and flowers, hand-fired roof tiles, carved woodwork, lattice windows, and pebbled courtyards.

When we visit Vancouver's Chinatown, we are amazed at the selection of noodles and tofu. Our Golden Tofu recipe (see next page) would be perfect, served cubed, as dim sum.

GOLDEN TOFU

1 cup (250 mL) sweet apple cider	1 tsp (5 mL) soy sauce	Olive oil (for brushing)
½ tsp (2 mL) ground ginger	¼ tsp (1 mL) garlic powder	
1½ Tbsp (23 mL) hoisin sauce	12 oz (340 g) extra-firm tofu	

IN A BOWL, combine all ingredients but the tofu.

Cut the tofu into ¾ inch (2 cm) thick slices. Place the slices into a flat dish. Pour the apple cider mixture over the tofu. Marinate for 2 hours in the refrigerator. Turn once while marinating.

Remove the tofu from the marinade. Set aside. Pour the apple cider marinade into a saucepan. Bring to a slow boil. Cook until it begins to thicken. Remove from the heat. Set aside.

Pat the tofu dry with paper towels.

Preheat the grill on medium-high (450–550°F/230–290°C) for 10 minutes with the lid closed. Using a pair of long-handled tongs, oil the grate by wiping it with a piece of folded paper towel dipped lightly in canola oil.

Brush olive oil on the tofu. Grill until browned, about 4–6 minutes per side, with the lid open. Brush the tofu with the marinade.

Transfer the tofu to a serving dish. Trickle with remaining marinade. Or, as an alternative, cover and chill the tofu in the refrigerator. Cut into cubes and toss in a salad.

A Garden of Scarecrows

IN 1984, JOE DELANEY decided to plant a garden in his field near Cheticamp, Nova Scotia. He lived 3 miles (5 kilometers) away from the site and worried that rabbits and deer would eat his vegetables. Joe built three scarecrows 6 feet (1.8 meters) high. He dressed them like humans and tied strips of plastic to their shoulders, wrists, and waists, to swing in the wind as a deterrent.

People suggested that Joe forget about growing a garden and cultivate more scarecrows. Encouraged by the attention, he mounted a total of 12 characters on posts by the end of the first summer. The following year, he expanded the group to 30. The variety of characters, from lumberjacks to recognizable international politicians, began to attract thousands of people every year.

In 1986, vandals struck and destroyed all of the scarecrows but one, whose name was Rory. Joe wrote about the experience in the local paper, describing the distressing night through Rory's eyes. Upon publication of the story, donations of money and scarecrow wardrobes arrived at his doorstep.

When we stopped for photographs, the scarecrows numbered around 100, Rory included. We signed a guestbook that recorded visitors from all over the world.

MINI PARSNIP PANCAKES

2 cups (500 mL) grated parsnips

1 cup (250 mL) finely chopped apple

1 cup (250 mL) finely chopped mild onion

½ cup (125 mL) all-purpose flour

2 eggs

1 tsp (5 mL) salt

½ tsp (2 mL) pepper

IN A BOWL, combine the parsnips, apple, and onion. Mix well. Add the flour and toss again.

In a separate bowl, combine the eggs, salt, and pepper. Whisk the egg mixture.

Add the egg mixture to the parsnip mixture. Stir to combine the wet and dry ingredients.

Place a griddle on the grill grate. Preheat the grill on medium-high (450–550°F/230–290°C) for 10 minutes. Using a pair of long-handled tongs, oil the griddle generously by wiping it with a piece of folded paper towel dipped in canola oil.

Test the heat by placing a soupspoon-sized dollop of parsnip mixture on the griddle. Gently flatten the surface of the pancake so the thickness is even. If one side is browned in 3 minutes, the griddle is at the right temperature. If the griddle is too hot or too cool, adjust the heat.

Continue spooning and flattening the remainder of the parsnip mixture onto the griddle. Grill for 3 minutes on each side. Oil the griddle as needed.

SMOKER-ROASTED CARAMELIZED TOMATOES

4 large tomatoes, cut into
4-5 slices each

Pinch of white sugar for each
tomato slice

Pinch of salt for each tomato slice

Pinch of pepper for each tomato slice

Pinch of dried oregano leaves
for each tomato slice

Pinch of grated Parmesan cheese
for each tomato slice

LINE A HEAVY metal baking sheet with aluminum foil. Rub or spray the foil
with olive oil.

Arrange the tomato slices in a single layer on the foil. Sprinkle the tomatoes
with sugar, salt, pepper, oregano, and Parmesan.

Preheat the smoker to medium-high (300°F/150°C), lid closed.

Place the baking sheet on the grate and roast the tomatoes about
2 hours or until the tomato slices start to turn brown at the edges and most of
the liquid around the tomatoes has caramelized.

Serve hot or cold, or on open-faced sandwiches and burgers.

FRUIT & DESSERT

Discovering a Sense of Place in Hawaii

EVEN THOUGH PINEAPPLE is synonymous with Hawaii, there is so much more fruit grown in the state's tropical climate. We could have spent all day at the roadside stands sampling dragon fruit, guava, papaya, starfruit, breadfruit, passion fruit, mangoes, coconuts, bananas, lychee, egg fruit (Hualālai), and others, but we were on the Big Island of Hawaii to visit the solidified lava beds of the last Hualālai volcanic eruption in 1801. The fruit stands would have to wait until later.

Miles of smooth black swirling lava, suspended in time, spread from the highway to the ocean. No grass, no trees, just waves of heat from the afternoon sun rising from the solid rock.

Ku'ulei Keakealani, the curator of the sacred site, welcomed us with a chant of soft, gentle rhythms. Our group formed a circle. Ku'ulei told us about her father, how her grandmother gave birth to him at the water's edge, just a mile from where we stood. A place where villagers once lived in temporary houses, fished, and gathered sea salt. Ku'ulei asked us to say our names and describe our personal places in the world. Every place was different, every story unique. A grandfather who took part in the Oklahoma land run. A Hawaiian-born mainlander who yearns to return some day. A Canadian raised on a farm, in the same house where her father was born.

We walked over the lava with Ku'ulei, to the ocean. We tasted natural sea salt, touched spiny sea urchins, and breathed in the salty scent of seaweed.

In the process of encouraging us to understand our own sense of place, Ku'ulei, the guardian of these sacred Hawaiian lava beds, shared her personal place with us. Her experience became ours, to take with us on our journey.

This day we learned about the real Hawaii beyond the beaches, the hotels, and the fruit stands.

PINEAPPLE SPEARS

1 pineapple, peeled, cored, and cut lengthwise into 8–10 spears

1 Tbsp (15 mL) extra-virgin olive oil

2 Tbsp (30 mL) honey

10 pinches of sea salt

⅛ tsp (0.5 mL) cayenne pepper

BRUSH THE PINEAPPLE spears lightly with olive oil. Sprinkle each spear with sea salt.

In a bowl, combine the honey and cayenne. Set aside.

Preheat the grill on medium (350–450°F/175–230°C) for 10 minutes with the lid closed. Using a pair of long-handled tongs, oil the grate by wiping it with a piece of folded paper towel dipped lightly in canola oil.

Place the pineapple spears on the grate. Grill for 4–5 minutes on each side with the lid open.

Transfer the pineapple spears to a plate.

Brush each spear with the honey-cayenne mixture.

PINEAPPLE & CANTALOUPE KABOBS

Twelve 1½-inch (4 cm) cubes fresh pineapple

Twelve 1½-inch (4 cm) cubes fresh cantaloupe

2 Tbsp (30 mL) butter, melted

1 Tbsp (15 mL) fresh lemon juice

1 Tbsp (15 mL) honey

¼ tsp (1 mL) ground cardamom

¼ tsp (1 mL) pepper

THREAD 3 PIECES of each fruit on each of 4 skewers, alternating pieces of pineapple and cantaloupe.

Place the kabobs in a flat dish.

In a bowl, combine the butter and remaining ingredients.

Brush the butter mixture over the kabobs. Refrigerate for 30 minutes before grilling.

Preheat the grill on high (550–600°F/290–315°C) for 10 minutes with the lid closed. Using a pair of long-handled tongs, oil the grate by wiping it with a piece of folded paper towel dipped lightly in canola oil. Reduce the heat to medium (350–450°F/175–230°C).

With the lid open, grill the fruit kabobs 4–5 minutes on each side.

Remove the kabobs from the grill. Serve immediately.

STRAWBERRY ORANGE TEMPTATION

2 cups (500 mL) sliced
fresh strawberries

2 Tbsp (30 mL) fresh orange juice

1 Tbsp (15 mL) storebought
balsamic glaze

1 Tbsp (15 mL) white sugar

4–6 scoops frozen orange sorbet

1 tsp (5 mL) orange zest

4 small sprigs rosemary

PLACE THE STRAWBERRY slices on a large piece of aluminum foil.

In a bowl, combine the orange juice, balsamic glaze, and sugar.

Drizzle the orange juice mixture over the strawberries.

Fold up the edges of the foil to make a tightly sealed packet.

Preheat the grill on medium (350–450°F/175–230°C) for 10 minutes.

Place the packet on the grate and cook for about 5 minutes or until the strawberries begin to sizzle.

Remove the packet from the grill. Transfer the strawberries and liquid to a bowl. Set aside to cool.

Spoon the strawberries and liquid over 4 individual servings of frozen orange sorbet.

Garnish with the orange zest and a sprig of rosemary. Serve immediately.

A Hobby Gone Wild

THE NEWFOUNDLAND INSECTARIUM in Reidville, north of Deer Lake, Newfoundland and Labrador, is the only private insectarium in Canada. The facility is the result of a hobby gone wild, a hobby of educating the public about insects.

In the butterfly pavilion, tropical butterflies thrive in a greenhouse-type setting. Brightly colored beauties glide through the air, rest on tropical leaves, and land on visitors' noses. The cathedral-like upstairs of the renovated dairy barn is abuzz with activity. It includes a beehive with 15,000 occupants, enclosed by glass for observation. A small red dot was placed on the queen's back so she can be easily seen.

As we watched the bee activity we learned a few bee basics. The queen bee rules, because she is the largest. The males are drones. Their only purpose before dying is to mate with the queen. The workers are female. There is only one queen and she is the only female to mate. When she dies, the males have nothing to do until a new queen is chosen so they fly out of the hive to spend time at the bee social club with their buddies. When a new queen is introduced, their club time is over.

When bees find nectar in flowers, they return to the hive and perform a dance to communicate the location of the nectar. A one-second dance means a third of a mile away, a six-second dance means almost two miles. The direction of the bee's dance points the direction to the nectar. A taste of the nectar denotes which flower was the source.

Lesson learned. When we are cooking and eating outdoors and one bee arrives to sample our food, we know it won't be long before she returns with what seems like the entire hive.

SYRUP-SEASONED MELON

1 firm cantaloupe

2 tsp (10 mL) cinnamon

1 tsp (5 mL) seasoned salt

¼ cup (60 mL) corn syrup

WASH THE OUTER skin of the cantaloupe. Cut the melon in half lengthwise. Remove the seeds.

Cut each half of the melon lengthwise into 6 wedges.

Preheat the grill on medium-high (450–550°F/230–290°C) with the lid closed. Using a pair of long-handled tongs, oil the grate by wiping it with a piece of folded paper towel dipped lightly in canola oil.

In a bowl, combine the corn syrup, cinnamon, and seasoned salt.

Brush one side of each wedge with the corn syrup mixture. Place the brushed side of the wedges on the grate to form grid marks. Grill for about 4 minutes with the lid closed.

Brush the corn syrup mixture over the top side of the wedges and turn the wedges over.

Grill the second side, with the lid closed, for about 4 minutes or until grid marks appear.

Arrange the grilled melon on a plate and brush with leftover corn syrup mixture.

BALSAMIC BLUE CHEESE PEACHES & PEARS

2 freestone peaches

2 pears

2 Tbsp (30 mL) white storebought balsamic glaze

1 tsp (5 mL) extra-virgin olive oil

Pinch of salt

4–6 tsp (20–30 mL) chunky blue cheese

WASH THE PEACHES and pears. Do not peel. Cut each one in half, lengthwise.

Remove the pits from the peaches. Cut the cores from the pears by scooping out the core with the tip of a spoon. Start at the wide end of the core. Leave the stem.

In a bowl, combine the balsamic glaze, oil, and salt. Mix well.

Preheat the grill on medium-high (450–550°F/230–290°C) for 10 minutes with the lid closed. Using a pair of long-handled tongs, oil the grate by wiping it with a piece of folded paper towel dipped lightly in canola oil.

Brush the peach and pear halves, inside and out, with the balsamic glaze mixture.

Place the peaches and pears on the grate, cavity-side down to form grid marks. Close the lid and grill for about 4 minutes.

Turn the fruit cavity-side up. Brush the cavity side with any remaining balsamic glaze mixture.

Spoon the blue cheese into the cavities. Close the lid and grill the fruit for another 2–3 minutes.

Serve the peaches and pears warm.

DATE-STUFFED APPLES

4 firm apples

4 tsp (20 mL) fresh orange zest

4 pitted dates, chopped into small pieces

4 tsp (20 mL) brown sugar

1 Tbsp (15 mL) butter

RINSE AND DRY the apples. Create a cavity in the apples, at least 1 inch (2.5 cm) wide, removing the cores with a paring knife or an apple corer. Leave the bottom ½ inch (1 cm) of the apples intact. If necessary, trim the apple bottoms so they stand flat on the counter.

Cut 2 pieces of heavy-duty aluminum foil into 12-inch (30 cm) squares. Brush the foil lightly with canola oil. Place 1 apple, open-side up, in the center of each square of foil.

Place the orange zest in the bottom of each apple pocket. Top the zest with dates, followed by the brown sugar. Melt the butter and pour it over the brown sugar.

Fold the foil up over the apples and seal tightly, allowing room for the apples to steam.

Preheat the grill for 10 minutes on low (250–300°F/120–150°C) with the lid closed.

Set the apple packets on the grate, filled side up.

Bake the apples, with the lid closed, for about 20 minutes or until the apples are tender.

Remove the packets from the grill and open the foil carefully to allow steam to escape.

Serve baked apples hot or cold.

Driving the Ocean Floor to Ministers Island

WE CANNOT MAKE a trip to New Brunswick without returning to the historic seaside resort town of St. Andrews. And we can't visit St. Andrews without making a side trip to Ministers Island. Part of the attraction is that at low tide, visitors can drive to the island across the ocean floor. Knowing that the tide will soon return and the strip of road will be underwater always adds an element of suspense. To add a little more trepidation to the experience, the time of high and low tides in the area shifts each day.

Ministers Island, named for an Anglican minister whose stone house still stands, is better known as the summer estate of Sir William Van Horne, the driving force in the construction of the Canadian Pacific Railway from the Atlantic to the Pacific.

Van Horne built a grand house and named it Covenhoven. Built in 1890 from local sandstone, Covenhoven has 50 rooms, 17 of which are bedrooms. There is a circular bathhouse, with a tidal swimming pool. In Van Horne's time, a windmill fed water to an underground storage tank. A gigantic livestock barn was home to thoroughbred horses and a prize herd of Dutch belted cattle. Fresh vegetables, exotic plants, peach trees, and grape vines grew in heated greenhouses. A creamery churned out butter. The story is that when Sir William was away from the island, fresh milk, butter, fruits, and vegetables from Covenhoven were delivered to him by railcar.

RUSTIC PEACH PIE

1 uncooked piecrust (found in the refrigerated section of grocery stores, or homemade)

6–8 unpeeled peaches

2 Tbsp (30 mL) melted butter

½ Tbsp (7.5 mL) white sugar

2 Tbsp (30 mL) brown sugar

COVER A COOKIE sheet with parchment paper. Place the piecrust flat on the parchment paper.

Cut the peaches into thin wedges and pile the fruit high in the center of the piecrust with the skin sides up for color. Leave about 1 inch (2.5 cm) of the crust uncovered around the rim.

Fold the edges of the dough up over the peaches, creasing the pastry as needed, to enclose the peaches except for a circle in the top center of the pie.

Preheat the grill on high (550–600°F/290–315°C) for 10 minutes with the lid closed.

Turn one side of the grill off and reduce the other side to medium (350–450°F/175–230°C) to maintain a temperature of about 375–400°F (190–200°C).

Brush the pastry with the melted butter and drizzle the remaining butter over the fruit.

Sprinkle the white sugar over the butter on the pastry. Sprinkle the brown sugar over the fruit.

Place the cookie sheet on the unlit side of the grate. Bake over indirect heat for about 50 minutes or until the crust is cooked through and golden brown. Rotate the pie halfway through baking time, if necessary, to prevent burning on one side.

Out-of-the-Ordinary Homes

NEAR VICTORIA, British Columbia, we toured a three-storey float home. The house was built on a cement-framed foam-filled foundation. The floating abode is tied to pylons that prevent it from lurching but at the same time allow it to sway gently up and down with the tide and current of the water. These float homes are ideal for urban dwellers who want to come home at the end of the day, park the car, step into the house for a change of clothes, and then step out the backdoor to a sailboat, powerboat, or dinghy tied up to the patio.

Just outside the entrance to Westbay Marine Village, we stopped to study a house on land that catches everyone's eye and camera. The old stucco structure is decorated, like a cake, in a nautical theme. Marine rope drapes below the roofline like batting. A giant seahorse garnishes one side of the front door, while a ship's mast and rigging with two figures in the crow's nest are on the other. A bird, possibly a stork, is delivering a baby over the chimney. We caught a glimpse of a whale around the side of the house. A dolphin, cannon, seagull, and anchor rest on the lawn.

And we thought that living in a motor home was out of the ordinary.

GRILLED POUND CAKE WITH ORANGES & CHOCOLATE

4 slices pound cake
(1 inch/2.5 cm thick)

¼ cup (60 mL) orange juice

½ cup (125 mL) mascarpone cheese

2 Tbsp (30 mL) icing sugar

2 Tbsp (30 mL) butter, softened

One 9-oz (256 mL) can mandarin oranges, drained

At least ½ cup (125 mL) chocolate syrup

PLACE THE SLICES of pound cake side by side on a plate. Using a fork, poke holes over the surface of each slice. Drizzle the orange juice over the cake slices.

Cover the slices with plastic wrap and refrigerate for 30 minutes.

Preheat the grill on medium-high (450–550°F/230–290°C) for 10 minutes with the lid closed. Using a pair of long-handled tongs, oil the grate by wiping it with a piece of folded paper towel dipped lightly in canola oil.

In a bowl, combine the mascarpone cheese with the icing sugar. Mix well. Set aside.

Spread the butter over both sides of the cake slices. Place the slices on the grate. Grill 1–2 minutes per side, with the lid open, to create grill marks.

Transfer the cake slices to a large platter. Cool for about 10 minutes.

With a knife, spread the mascarpone cheese over the upper surface of each slice.

Arrange mandarin orange segments over the mascarpone cheese. Drizzle with chocolate syrup.

MAKES 6–8 SERVINGS

APPLE PIE IN A CAST IRON FRYING PAN

2 apples, peeled, cored, and thinly sliced

1 tsp (5 mL) lemon juice

One 18-oz (511 mL) can apple pie filling

½ cup (125 mL) butter

¼ cup (60 mL) brown sugar

½ tsp (2 mL) ground cinnamon

1 uncooked piecrust (found in the refrigerated section of grocery store, or homemade)

1 tsp (5 mL) white sugar

PREHEAT THE GRILL on medium (350–450°F/175–230°C) for 10 minutes with the lid closed.

Peel and core the apples. Cut the apples into thin slices. Toss in a bowl with the lemon juice.

Add the apple pie filling to the apple slices. Stir to mix together.

Melt the butter and stir in the brown sugar and cinnamon. Set 2 Tbsp (30 mL) aside and pour the rest of the butter mixture into the bottom of a cast iron frying pan.

Add the apple mixture to the frying pan.

Place the piecrust over the mixture in the frying pan.

Tuck the sides of the pastry tightly around the inside of the pan to completely cover the filling. Poke several holes in the pastry with a fork.

Brush the remaining 2 Tbsp (30 mL) butter mixture over the top of the pastry. Sprinkle the pastry with white sugar.

Turn one side of the grill off and leave the other side on medium heat to maintain a temperature of about 350–375°F (175–190°C). Place the frying pan on the unlit side of the grill.

Close the lid and bake the pie for about 50 minutes or until the crust is browned and the pie is bubbling. If one side of the crust is browning too quickly, rotate the pan.

Using a heat-resistant glove, remove the frying pan from the grill and set on a heat resistant surface to cool before slicing.

ACCESSORIES TO THE RECIPES

EASTERN NORTH CAROLINA MOPPING SAUCE

2 cups (500 mL) apple cider vinegar

1 cup (250 mL) white vinegar

¼ cup (60 mL) water

1 Tbsp (15 mL) white sugar

1 tsp (5 mL) hot sauce

1 tsp (5 mL) crushed red pepper

½ tsp (2 mL) salt

IN A JAR with a tight-fitting lid, combine all ingredients.

Shake well to blend the flavors.

Refrigerate for several hours and shake again before using.

This sauce can be stored in a sealed container in the refrigerator for 2 weeks.

MOLASSES SAUCE

½ cup (125 mL) chopped onion

3 garlic cloves, finely chopped

1 Tbsp (15 mL) canola oil

¼ cup (60 mL) molasses

¼ cup (60 mL) ketchup

2 Tbsp (30 mL) apple cider vinegar

1 Tbsp (15 mL) Worcestershire sauce

1 Tbsp (15 mL) Dijon mustard

1 tsp (5 mL) coarsely ground pepper

½ tsp (2 mL) salt

IN A SAUCEPAN, cook and stir the onions and garlic in the canola oil over medium heat until the onions are tender.

In a bowl, combine the remaining ingredients. Mix well.

Stir the molasses mixture into the saucepan. Bring to a boil over medium-high heat. Reduce heat to medium and stir for 5 minutes.

Cover and refrigerate until ready to use.

This sauce can be stored in a sealed container in the refrigerator for 1 week.

MAKES ⅔ CUP (160 ML)

SMOKED GARLIC AIOLI

2 whole heads of garlic

½ cup (125 mL) good quality mayonnaise

2 tsp (10 mL) Dijon mustard

2 tsp (10 mL) fresh lemon juice

Pinch of pepper

CUT THE TOPS off the whole heads of garlic to expose the tips of the garlic cloves. Brush the outside skin of the garlic with olive oil.

Preheat the smoker to medium-high (300°F/150°C), lid closed.

Cook the garlic, cut side up on the grate, for about 1 hour.

Transfer the garlic from the smoker to a cutting board.

When cool enough to touch, squeeze the soft flesh out of the garlic skin. Discard the skin.

Finely chop the flesh. Transfer to a bowl.

Add the remaining ingredients to the garlic. Blend until smooth.

Cover and refrigerate until ready to use.

This sauce can be stored in a sealed container in the refrigerator for 3–4 days.

MAKES ABOUT 1¼ CUPS (310 ML)

MEMPHIS-STYLE DRY RUB

½ cup (125 mL) paprika

2 Tbsp (30 mL) brown sugar

2 Tbsp (30 mL) white sugar

1 Tbsp (15 mL) garlic powder

1 Tbsp (15 mL) onion powder

1 Tbsp (15 mL) celery salt

2 tsp (10 mL) cayenne pepper

2 tsp (10 mL) dry mustard

1 tsp (5 mL) mustard seeds

1 tsp (5 mL) ground allspice

1 tsp (5 mL) dried thyme leaves

1 tsp (5 mL) sea salt

1 tsp (5 mL) pepper

IN A BOWL, combine all ingredients. Mix well.

Store in an airtight container in a cool, dry place for up to 1 month.

231 | ACCESSORIES TO THE RECIPES

MANGO SALSA

1 mango, peeled and diced

¼ cup (60 mL) finely diced red onion

2 Roma tomatoes, diced

½ jalapeno pepper, seeds removed, finely chopped

¼ cup (60 mL) chopped fresh cilantro

IN A GLASS bowl, combine all ingredients. Stir well.

Cover and refrigerate until ready to use.

This salsa can be stored in a sealed container in the refrigerator for 2–3 days.

SOUTHWEST SALSA

1 chipotle pepper in adobo sauce

¾ cup (185 mL) corn niblets

¾ cup (185 mL) black beans

2 fresh plum tomatoes, diced

¼ cup (60 mL) chopped red onion

2 cloves garlic, chopped

3 Tbsp (45 mL) chopped fresh cilantro

½ tsp (2 mL) salt

2 Tbsp (30 mL) fresh lime juice

1 Tbsp (15 mL) extra-virgin olive oil

REMOVE THE SEEDS and membrane from the chipotle pepper. Finely chop the pepper.

In a bowl, combine all ingredients. Mix well.

Cover and refrigerate until ready to use.

This salsa can be stored in a sealed container in the refrigerator for 2–3 days.

POULTRY BRINE

4 cups (1 L) water

¼ cup (60 mL) sea salt

¼ cup (60 mL) white sugar

1 tsp (5 mL) celery seed

½ tsp (2 mL) anise seed

½ tsp (2 mL) mustard seed

½ tsp (2 mL) whole black peppercorns

¼ tsp (1 mL) ground coriander

1 whole allspice

½ cinnamon stick

½ bay leaf

¼ lemon

IN A POT, combine all ingredients.

Bring to a boil over medium-high heat.

Boil for 5 minutes.

Remove and discard the cinnamon stick, bay leaf, and lemon.

Cool the brine before using.

BASIC GRILLING PIZZA DOUGH

1 cup (250 mL) warm water

2½ cups (625 mL) bread flour, divided

2¼ tsp (11 mL) active dry yeast

½ Tbsp (7.5 mL) white sugar

½ Tbsp (7.5 mL) salt

2 Tbsp (30 mL) extra-virgin olive oil

IN A BOWL, combine the warm water, ½ cup (125 mL) flour, yeast, and sugar. Stir well and let sit until the mixture is foamy and bubbling, about 20 minutes.

In a separate bowl, combine the remaining 2 cups (500 mL) flour and the salt. Add the flour mixture to the yeast mixture. While stirring the flour into the yeast mixture, trickle the olive oil into the bowl. Stir until the dough holds together.

Turn the dough onto a lightly floured board. Knead the dough, adding small amounts of flour from the board until the dough is soft and slightly sticky.

Form the dough into a ball and place in a large bowl. Spread the oil over the entire ball. Cover the bowl with a cloth until doubled in size, about 2 hours.

Place the dough on a floured cutting board and cut into 3 equal portions.

Dough can be made to this stage and frozen. To freeze, brush the dough portions with olive oil and place them in individual resealable plastic bags. When ready to use, thaw the frozen dough overnight in the refrigerator. Before using, place the dough in a bowl brushed with olive oil and let sit for 30 minutes at room temperature.

For grilling instructions and topping ideas see Sun-Dried Tomato & Artichoke Pizza (see page 59) and Caprese Pizza (see page 61).

ACKNOWLEDGEMENTS

THANK YOU TO all of you who help and inspire us daily, whether it is feeding our creativity, taste testing our finished dishes, sharing our passion for travel, or making us feel at home in your community. We are grateful for farmers, fishers, vintners, creative chefs, restaurateurs, tourism representatives, and far-flung friends for giving freely of your time and expertise to show us the bounty and beauty of your corners of the world. We have shared special meals, stimulating conversations, good wine, and camaraderie with you.

We are thankful for each other and our shared vision, without which we could not have traveled so far and accomplished so much.

We treasure our good neighbors at the test kitchen and our family and friends. Thank you for understanding that we really were in cookbook quarantine and couldn't come out to play.

Thank you, Traeger Canada for your continued support. The Traeger Lil' Tex Pro smoker performed beautifully, allowing us to relax and be creative. Thank you, Napoleon. Our Prestige 500 grill provided powerful reliability and versatility. Thank you, Schinkels' Gourmet Meats. Good grilling begins with good meat.

Thank you, Whitecap Books.

INDEX